Rockschool Band Bass Companion Guide

Welcome to the Rockschool BBK Companion Guide	3
Technical Exercises	4
Sight Reading (Grades D–5)	60
Improvisation & Interpretation (Grades 1–5)	78
Ear Tests (Grades D–5)	94
General Musicianship Questions (Grades D–5)	120

www.rockschool.co.uk

Acknowledgements

Published by Rockschool Ltd. © 2010

Catalogue Number: RSK051001

ISBN Number: 9781902775876

Written by: Jeremy Ward

Compiled by: Jeremy Ward, James Uings and Simon Troup

Edited by: James Uings & Jeremy Ward

Music engraving and layouts: Simon & Jennie Troup *www.digitalmusicart.com*

Audio production: Jason Woolley *jasonwooleymusic.co.uk*

Mastered by: Duncan Jordan

Syllabus Director: Jeremy Ward

Cover design: *www.fuelcreativity.com*

Printed and bound in the United Kingdom by Caligraving Ltd, Thetford, Norfolk

CDs manufactured in the United Kingdom by brandedmedia *www.brandedmedia.net*

Exclusive Distributors: Music Sales Ltd *www.musicroom.com*

Visit the Rockschool website at *www.rockschool.co.uk*

Telephone: +44 (0)845 460 4747

Fax: +44 (0)845 460 1960

Welcome to the Rockschool BBK Companion Guide

Welcome to the Rockschool *Companion Guide* for Band Based Keyboards. This *Companion Guide* is designed to give teachers, learners and candidates multiple examples of the unseen tests that are to be found within each Rockschool grade exam from Grades Debut to 5. The *Companion Guide* contains six examples of each of the following tests:

- Sight Reading (Grades D–5)
- Improvisation & Interpretation (Grades 1–5)*
- Ear Tests (Grades D–5)*

All of the test examples marked (*) can be found on the audio CDs accompanying this *Companion Guide*. Please refer to the track listings given in the text.

You will also find examples of the kinds of general musicianship questions that candidates are asked in each grade exam from Grades Debut–5. The technical exercises have also been printed in full.

Each section of the book starts with an introduction that includes tips on making the most of your practise time and advice on how to approach the tests in the exam.

Teachers, learners and candidates should also refer to the Rockschool Syllabus Guide for Band Based Keyboards where they will find the technical specifications for each section of the exam syllabus, including those parts (the performance pieces) not covered by this *Companion Guide*.

The purpose of the *Companion Guide* is to give candidates practice examples of the kinds of tests they will encounter in the exam. In the case of the sight reading, improvisation & interpretation and ear tests, we have created examples within each grade that offer candidates a progressive level of difficulty within a single grade: the first test example will be relatively simple when compared with the actual tests used in the exam, while the last example will be relatively more difficult. We have done this with the aim of aiding candidate confidence when faced with the tests in the exam.

If you have any queries about the syllabus for band based keyboards (or any other exam syllabus offered by Rockschool in guitar, bass guitar, drums, vocals, piano or our Music Practitioners qualifications) then please do not hesitate to call us on +44 (0)845 460 4747 or email us at: **info@rockschool.co.uk**. The Rockschool website, **www.rockschool.co.uk**, has detailed information on all aspects of our examinations, including examination regulations, detailed marking schemes and marking criteria as well as handy tips on how to get the most out of the performance pieces.

Technical Exercises

In this section, the examiner will ask you to play a selection of exercises. These contain examples of the kinds of scales and chords you can use when playing the pieces. At Grades 4 & 5 you will also be asked to play exercises based on different seventh chords. All grades require the preparation of a riff exercise to be played to a CD backing track.

Practice and preparation of scales

Scales are crucial to a keyboardist's technical and musical development. It's important to find interesting, stimulating ways to play them to avoid uninteresting practice sessions that lots of players associate with scales.

Selecting fingerings

Some scales, like the major scale, have an accepted set of standard fingerings. Some, like the pentatonic scale, have several acceptable fingerings.

1. C major scale | Right hand fingering

2. C major scale | Left hand fingering

3. A minor pentatonic scale | Right hand fingerings

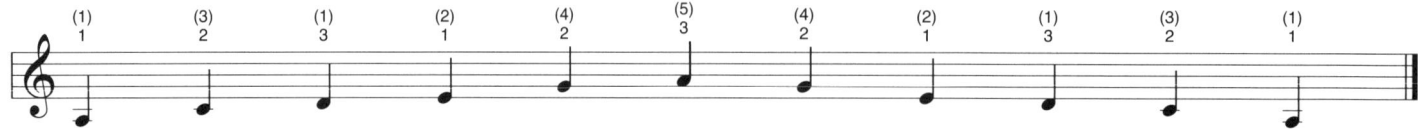

Spend time finding a fingering that suits your size and shape of hand. Once you have the right one for you, stick to it. Changing will cause uncertainty and lead to frustration, which will make you less likely to practise.

When you have settled on your fingering, practise the scales in different ways. This achieves two things: it maintains interest by keeping the brain working (mental memory) and it helps develop finger memory (muscular memory). Both forms of memory contribute to fluent, confident playing.

Securing fingerings

A good way to start is to play the notes played by the thumb separately and then all other notes as a chord. This exercise doesn't sound particularly pleasant, but it establishes which notes should be played with the thumb. There is a tendency to move the thumb stiffly and with a heavy attack. Make sure the thumb is even and relaxed. Remember: the thumb bends at several joints like all the other fingers.

4. Securing major scale right hand fingering

5. Securing major scale left hand fingering

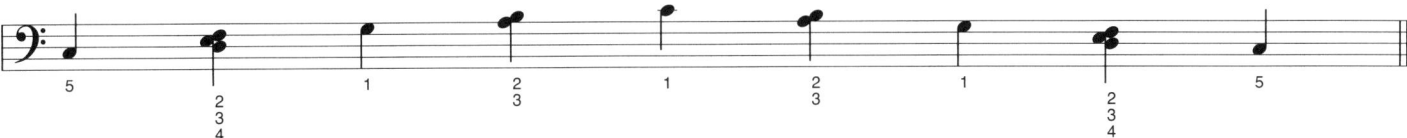

6. Securing minor pentatonic right hand fingering

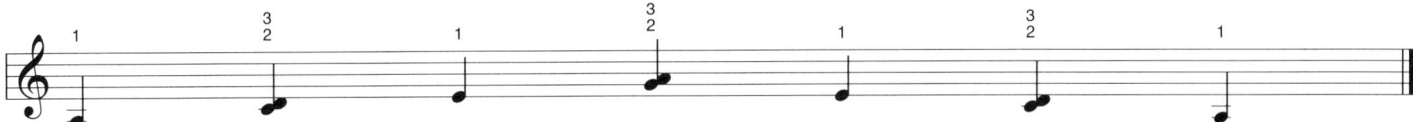

Another good way to vary your scale practise is to play them 'hands separately' switching hands at the octave. This helps secure scale fingerings for both hands. Ensure the 'takeover' between hands is smooth. Example 7 shows the exercise with both hands playing in the same octave, but you should also practise scales with each hand playing in different octaves.

7. Major scale | Hands separately | Alternating hands

Rhythmic variations

When you feel comfortable with your scale fingerings, practise using different rhythms. The rhythmic variations mean that extra concentration is required because the emphasis on changing fingers is put in different places in the music. As a result, finger memory is strengthened. The result is even, fluent scales.

8. Major scale | Hands together with rhythmic variation

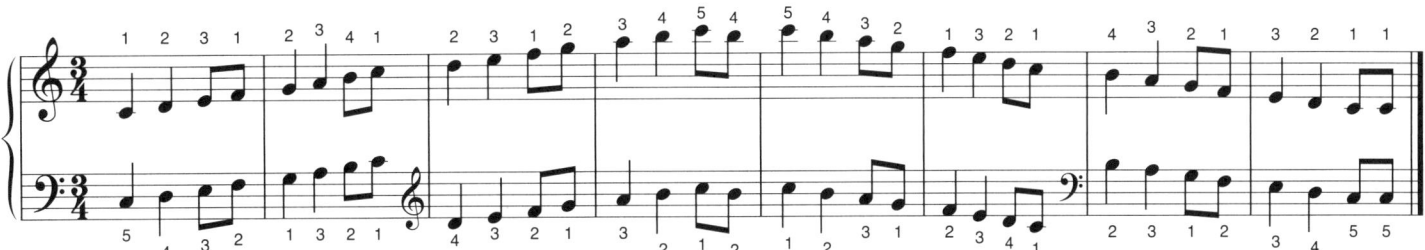

9. Major scale | Hands together with rhythmic variation

10. Major scale | Hands together with rhythmic variation

11. Major scale | Hands together with rhythmic variation

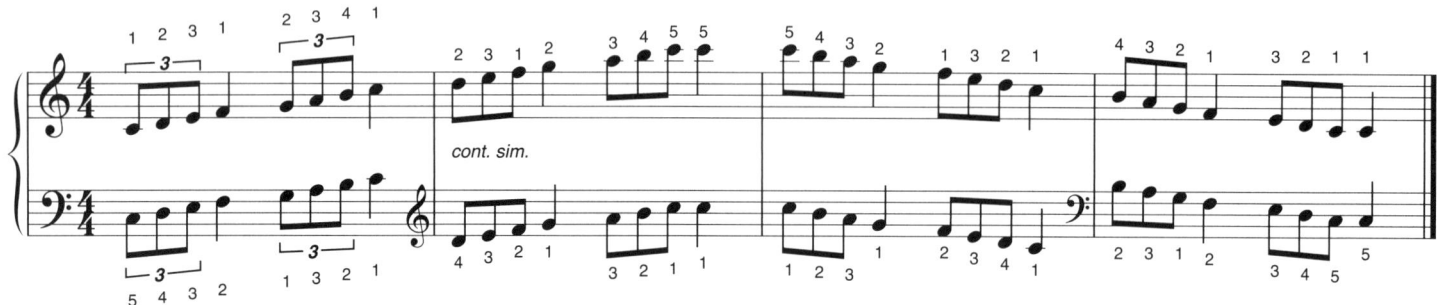

Combining scales and chords

A more advanced exercise is to play chords in one hand and scales in the other. The following examples place chords in both the left and right hands. This is a challenging exercise, so you may wish to work on each hand individually before playing the examples as written.

12. Major scale with chords I & IV in the left hand

13. Major scale with chords I & IV in the right hand

14. Major scale with chords I & V in the right hand

Different scales played simultaneously with different hands

Finally, for the ultimate challenge, and only when you are feeling really confident, play two scales in different keys at the same time.

15. C major and E♭ major scales played simultaneously with different hands

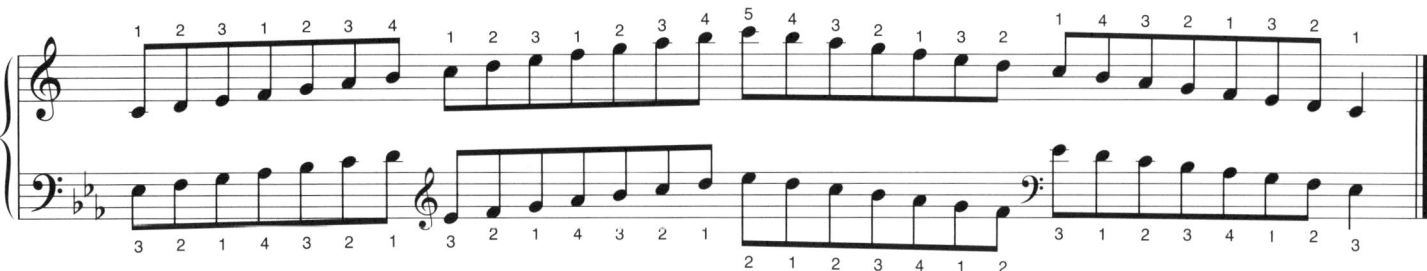

16. C major and A natural minor scales played simultaneously with different hands

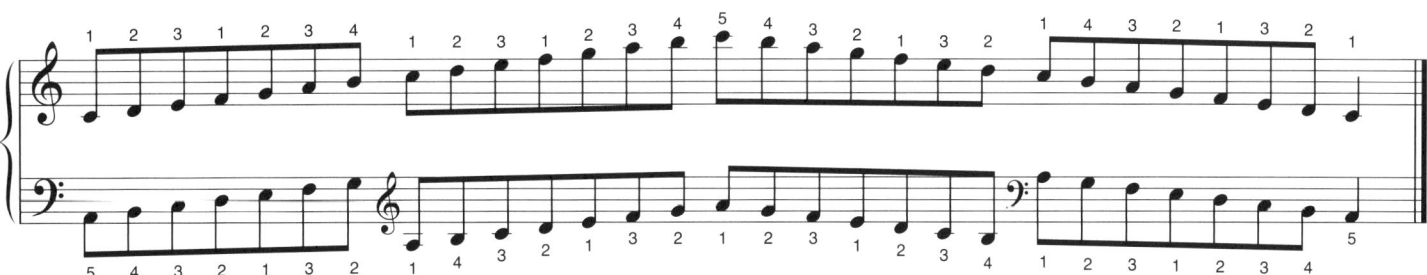

The Exam

The examiner will ask if you want to do the Technical Exercises (scales and chords) or the performance pieces first in the exam. Most candidates opt for the pieces as they are invariably the best rehearsed and most enjoyable. However, you should *consider playing the scales first*. They are short, so you are not playing for very long at one time and this can help settle your nerves.

The examiner will offer you the metronome for the entire scale or just as a four-beat lead in. Choose the one that is most comfortable and that you are used to practising. It's a bad idea to change on exam day!

The examiner will be looking for three key elements:

- Prompt response. Make sure you are thoroughly prepared and can begin immediately
- An even tempo. Lots of candidates speed up on the descent as they see the end in sight and rush towards it. Practise staying at the same tempo - a metronome can help with this.
- Accuracy and evenness. Ensure that the scale flows and that there are no delays as the thumb passes under the rest of the hand.

Technical Exercises

Debut

In this section, the examiner will ask you to play a selection of exercises drawn from each of the three groups shown below. Groups A and B contain examples of the kinds of scales and chords you can use when playing the pieces in the BBK Debut candidate book. In Group C you will be asked to prepare the riff exercise and play it to the CD backing track. You do not need to memorise the exercises, and *while you cannot take this book into the exam* you can use the BBK Debut candidate book. The examiner will be looking for a prompt and accurate response, fluency and consistency of pulse.

The examiner will give you the tempo in the exam. All scales and chords should be played using the piano patch.

Group A: Scales | Minor pentatonic scales | ♩=70

All scales are to be prepared right hand only.

1a. A minor pentatonic scale

1b. E minor pentatonic scale

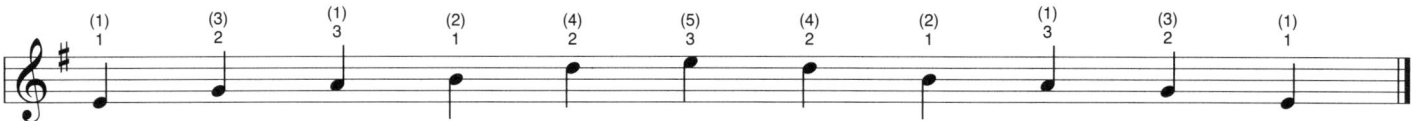

1c. C major scale

Group B: Chords | ♩=70

All chord sequences should be played with the right or left hand as directed by the examiner.
Left hand may be played an octave higher than written.

1a. Chords i and iv in A minor | Right hand

1b. Chords i and iv in A minor | Left hand

Technical Exercises

2a. Chords i and v in A minor | Right hand

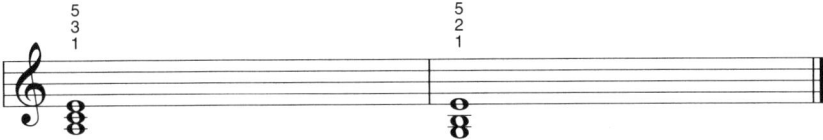

2b. Chords i and v in A minor | Left hand

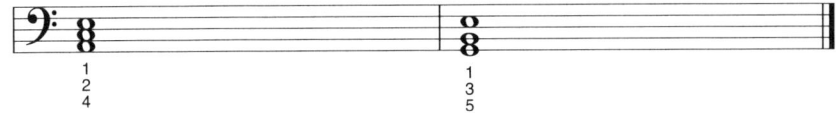

3a. Chords I and IV in C major | Right hand

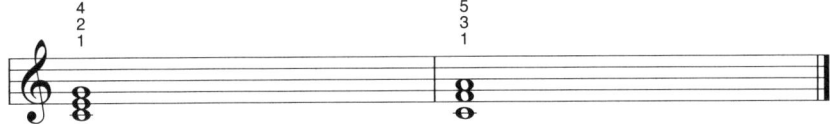

3b. Chords I and IV in C major | Left hand

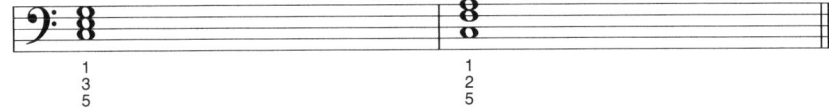

4a. Chords I and V in C major | Right hand

4b. Chords I and V in C major | Left hand

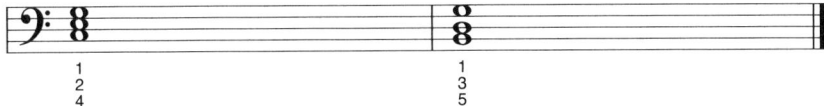

Group C: Riff | ♩=90

In the exam you will be asked to play the following riff to the backing track found on the BBK candidate book CD. The riff pattern shown in bar 1 should be played in the following bars using the nearest right hand inversions for the stated chords, referring to Group B above where necessary. The root notes of the chords to be played are shown in each bar.

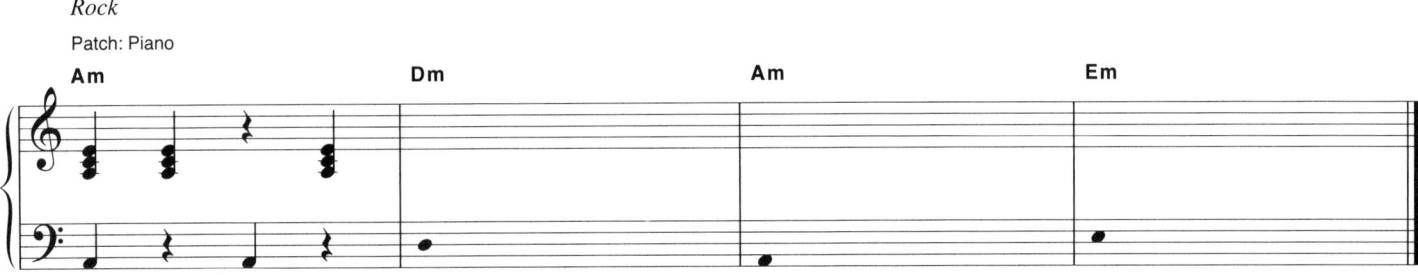

Technical Exercises

Grade 1

In this section, the examiner will ask you to play a selection of exercises drawn from each of the three groups shown below. Groups A and B contain examples of the kinds of scales and chords you can use when playing the pieces in the BBK Grade 1 candidate book. In Group C you will be asked to prepare the riff exercise and play it to the CD backing track. You do not need to memorise the exercises, and *while you cannot take this book into the exam* you can use the BBK Grade 1 candidate book. The examiner will be looking for a prompt and accurate response, fluency and consistency of pulse.

The examiner will give you the tempo in the exam. All scales and chords should be played using the piano patch.

Group A: Scales | Minor pentatonic scales | ♩=80

All scales are to be prepared hands separately.

1a. A minor pentatonic scale

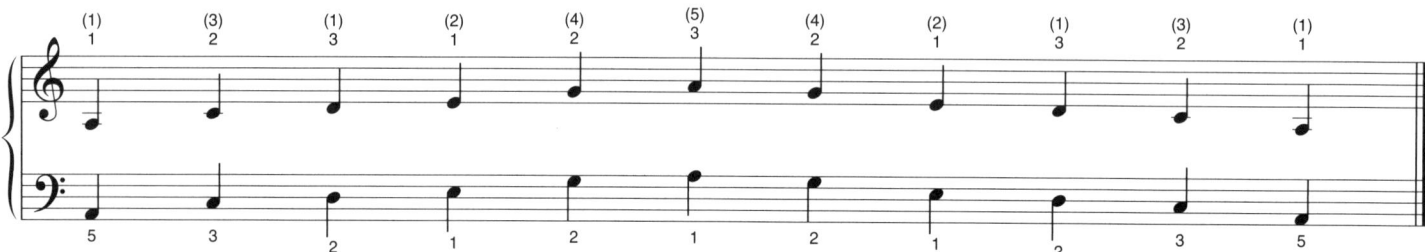

1b. E minor pentatonic scale

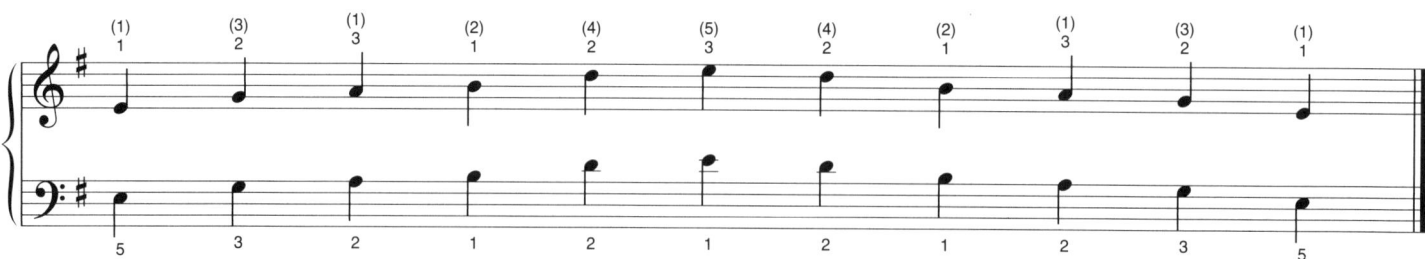

Group A: Scales | Major scales | ♩=80

All scales are to be prepared hands separately.

2a. C major scale

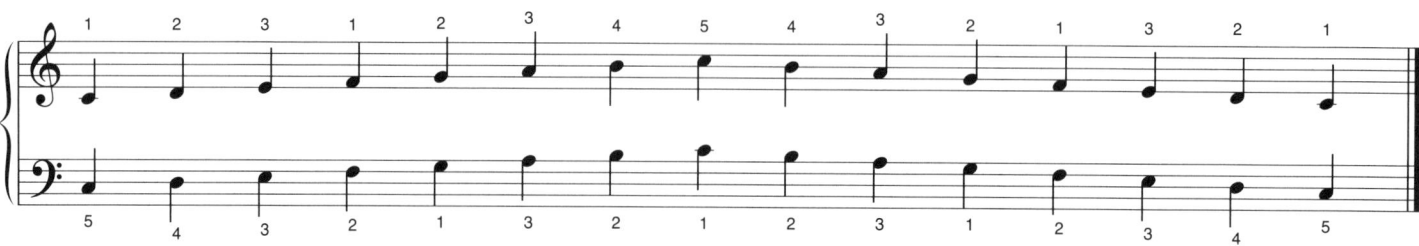

2b. G major scale

Technical Exercises

Group B: Chords | Chords i and iv in minor keys | ♩=60

All chord sequences should be played with the right or left hand as directed by the examiner.

1a. Chords i and iv in A minor

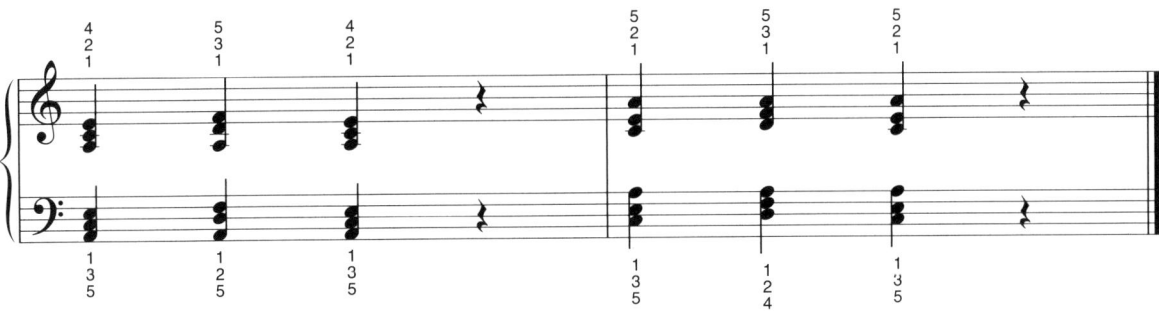

1b. Chords i and iv in E minor

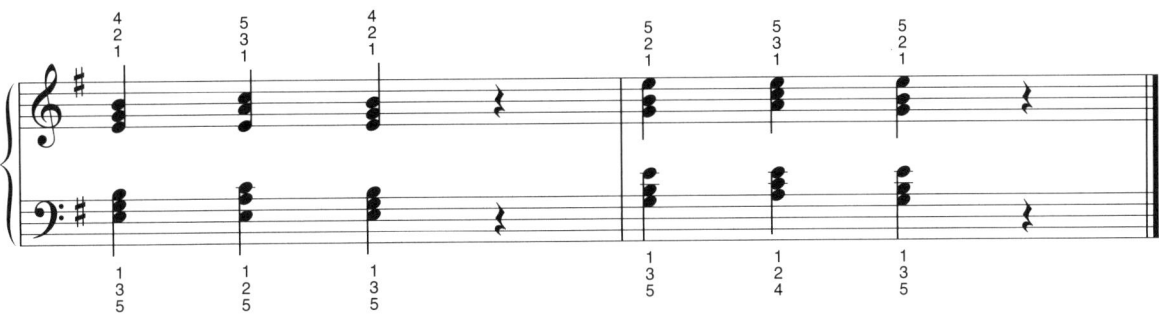

Group B: Chords | Chords i and v in minor keys | ♩=60

All chord sequences should be played with the right or left hand as directed by the examiner.

2a. Chords i and v in A minor

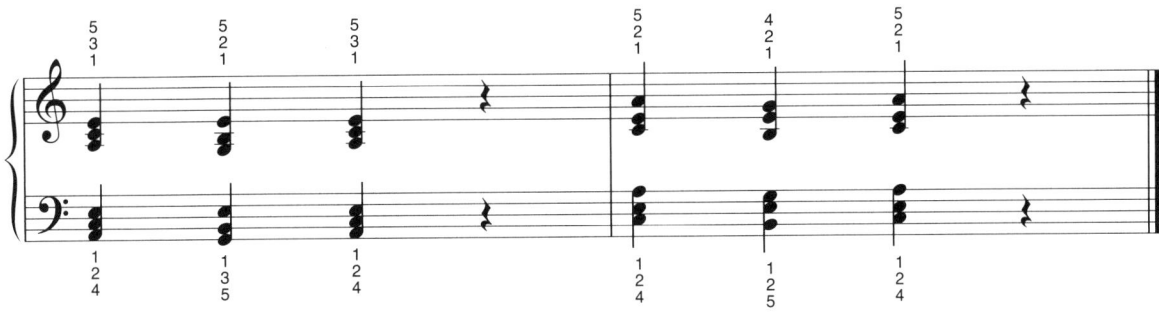

2b. Chords i and v in E minor

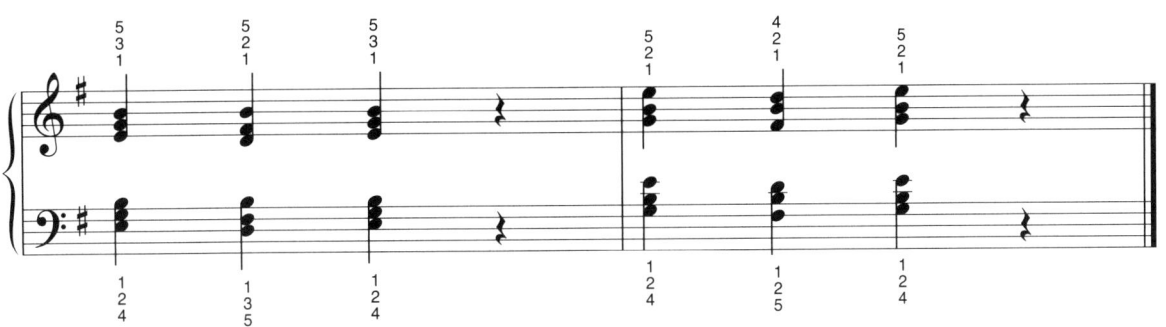

Technical Exercises

Group B: Chords | Chords I and IV in major keys | ♩=60

All chord sequences should be played with the right or left hand as directed by the examiner.

3a. Chords I and IV in C major

3b. Chords I and IV in G major

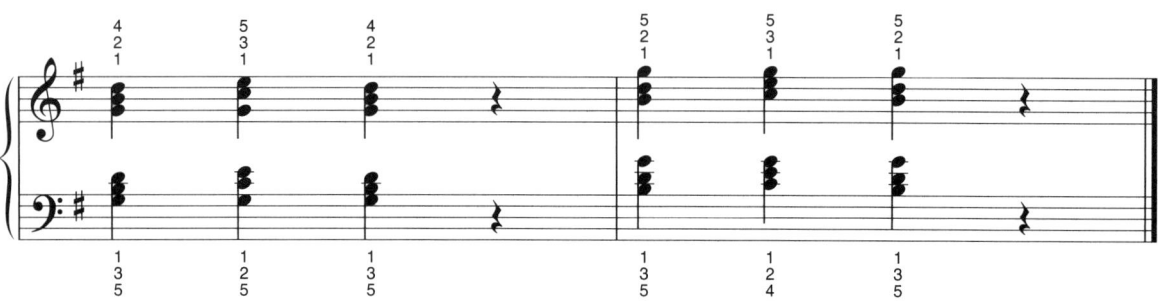

Group B: Chords | Chords I and V in major keys | ♩=60

All chord sequences should be played with the right or left hand as directed by the examiner.

4a. Chords I and V in C major

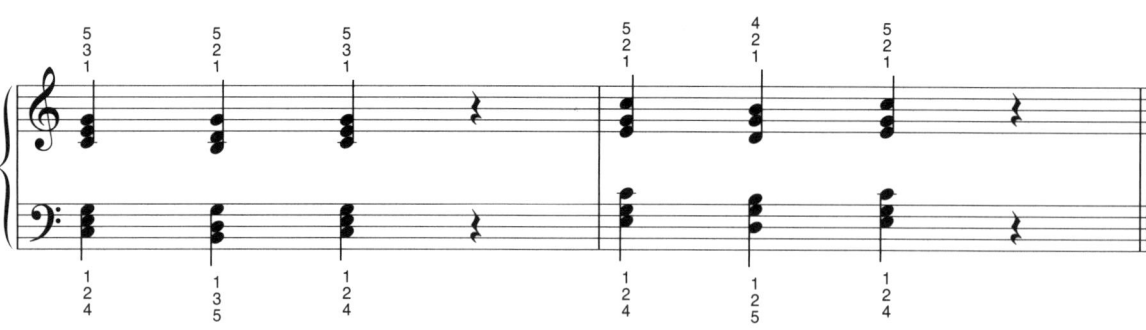

4b. Chords I and V in G major

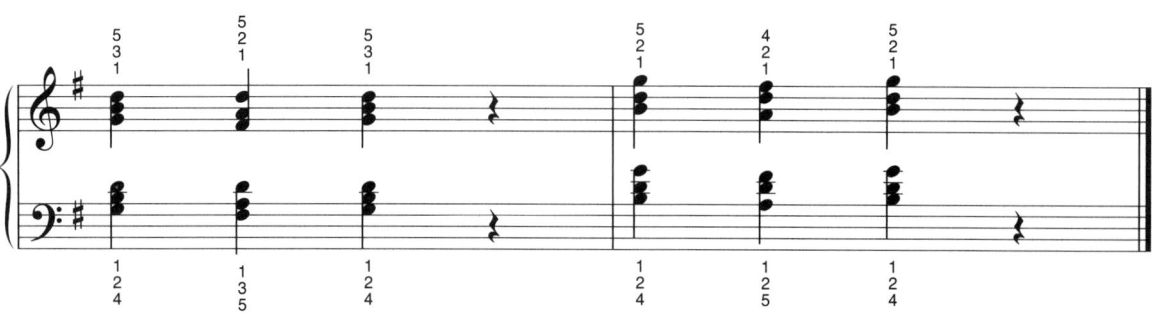

Technical Exercises

Group C: Riff | ♩=90

In the exam you will be asked to play the following riff to the backing track found on the BBK candidate book CD. The riff pattern shown in bar 1 should be played in the following bars using the nearest right hand inversions for the stated chords, referring to Group B above where necessary. The root notes of the chords to be played are shown in each bar.

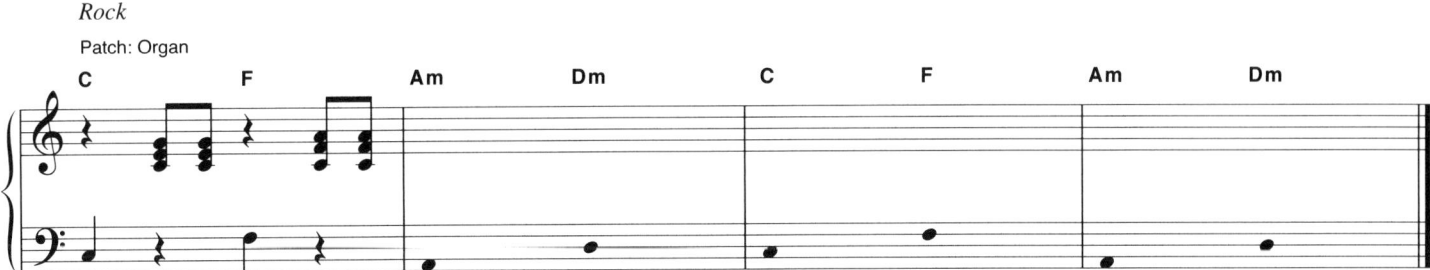

Technical Exercises

Grade 2

In this section, the examiner will ask you to play a selection of exercises drawn from each of the three groups shown below. Groups A and B contain examples of the kinds of scales and chords you can use when playing the pieces in the BBK Grade 2 candidate book. In Group C you will be asked to prepare the riff exercise and play it to the CD backing track. You do not need to memorise the exercises, and *while you cannot take this book into the exam* you can use the BBK Grade 2 candidate book. The examiner will be looking for a prompt and accurate response, fluency and consistency of pulse.

The examiner will give you the tempo in the exam. All scales and chords should be played using the piano patch.

Group A: Scales | Minor pentatonic scales | ♩=100

All scales are to be prepared hands separately.

1a. A minor pentatonic scale

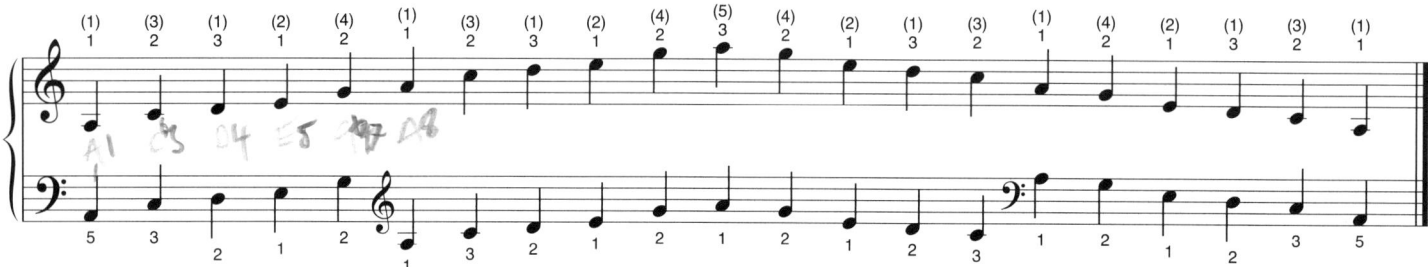

1b. D minor pentatonic scale

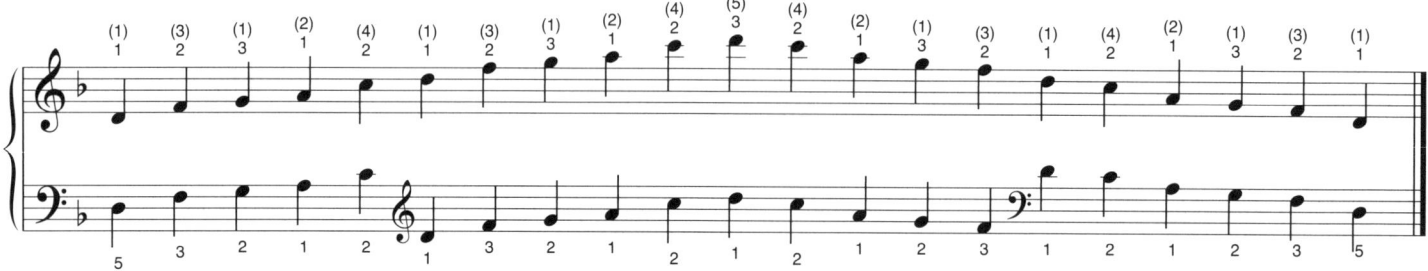

1c. E minor pentatonic scale

Technical Exercises

Group A: Scales | Natural minor scales | ♩=100

All scales are to be prepared hands separately.

2a. A natural minor scale

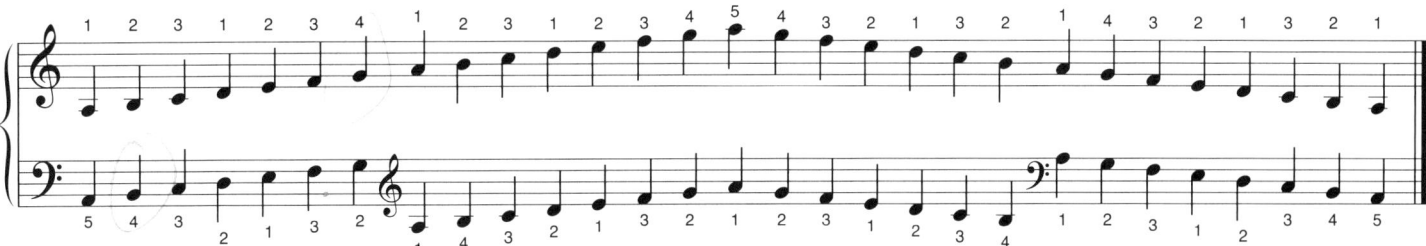

2b. D natural minor scale

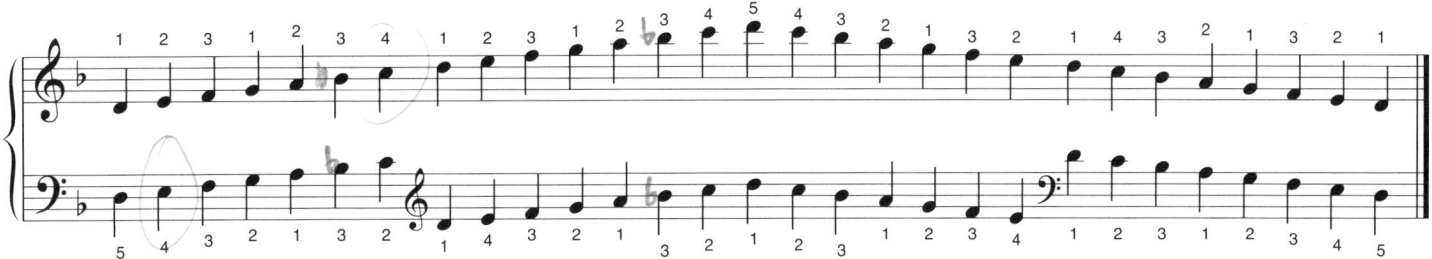

2c. E natural minor scale

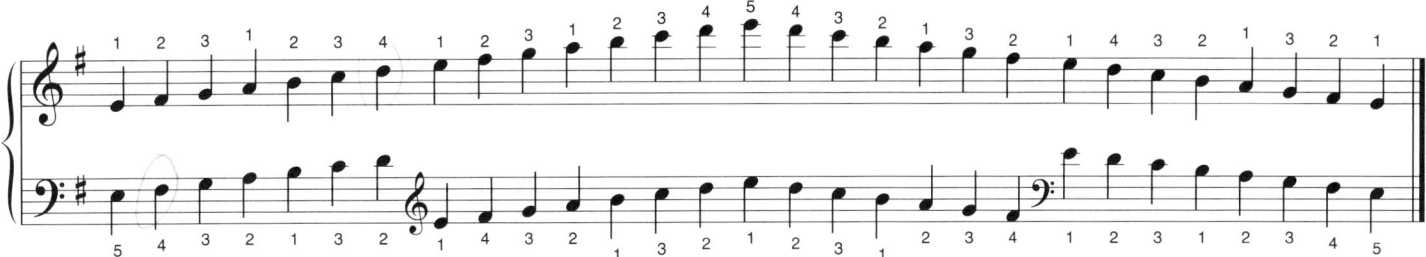

Technical Exercises

Group A: Scales | Major scales | ♩=100

All scales are to be prepared hands separately.

3a. C major scale

3b. G major scale

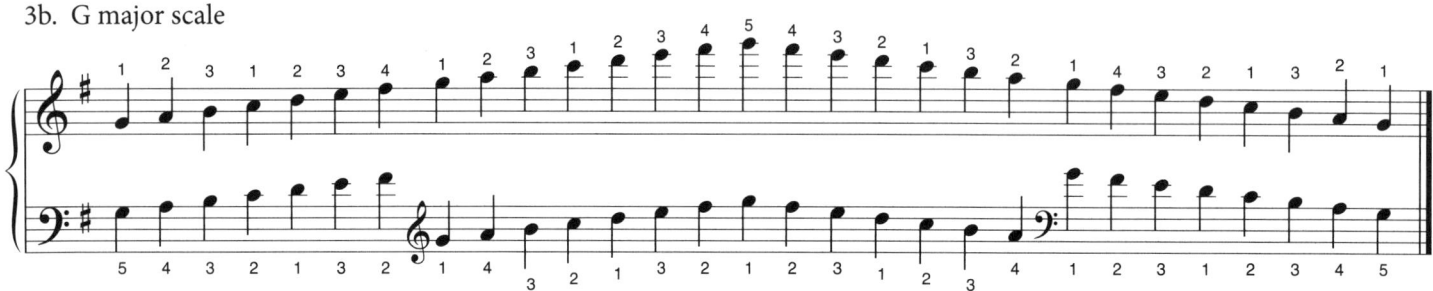

3c. D major scale

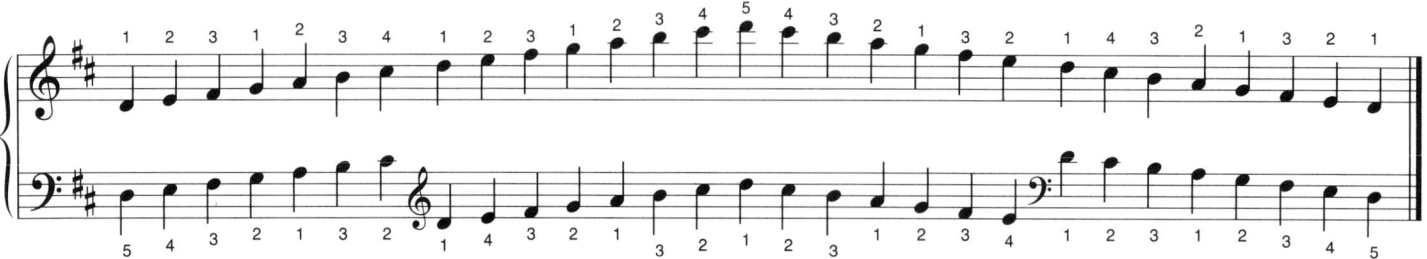

3d. F major scale

Technical Exercises

Group B: Chords | Chord sequence 1 | ♩=60

All chord sequences should be played with the right or left hand as directed by the examiner.

1a. Chord sequence in A minor

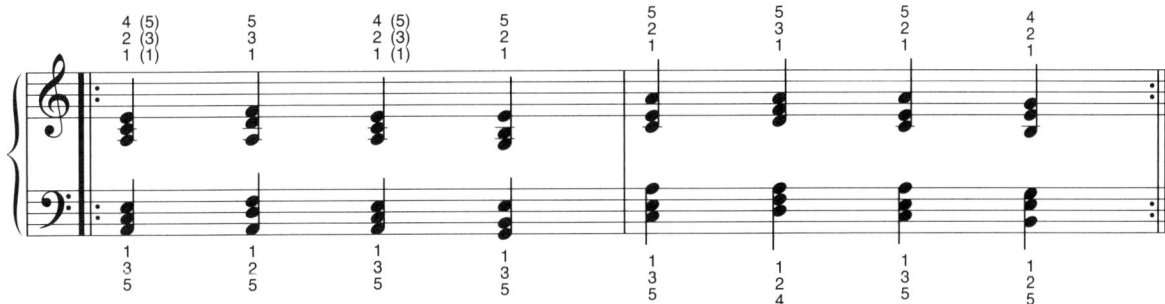

1b. Chord sequence in D minor

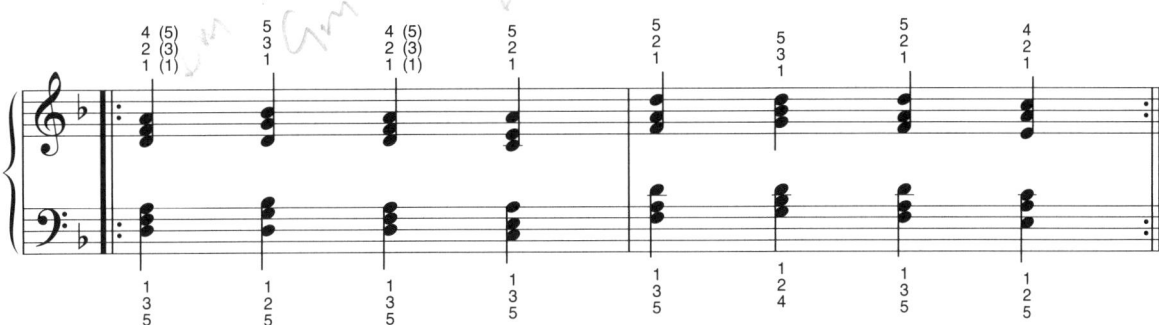

1c. Chord sequence in E minor

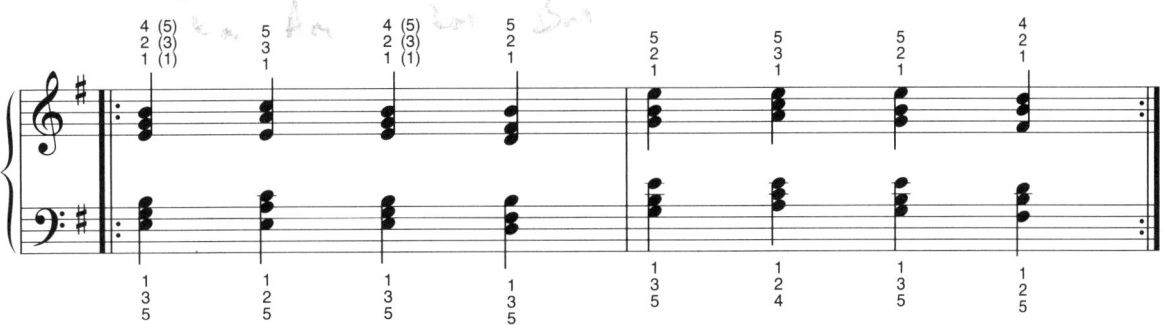

Technical Exercises

Group B: Chords | Chord sequence 2 | ♩=60

All chord sequences should be played with the right or left hand as directed by the examiner.

2a. Chord sequence in C major

2b. Chord sequence in G major

2c. Chord sequence in D major

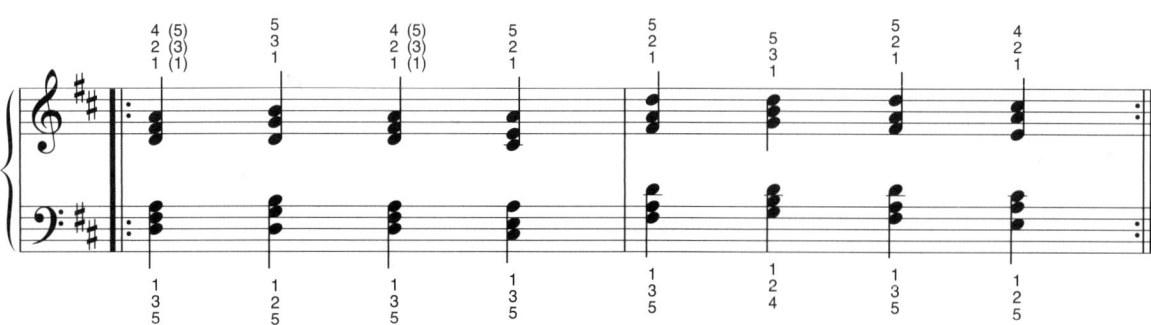

2d. Chord sequence in F major

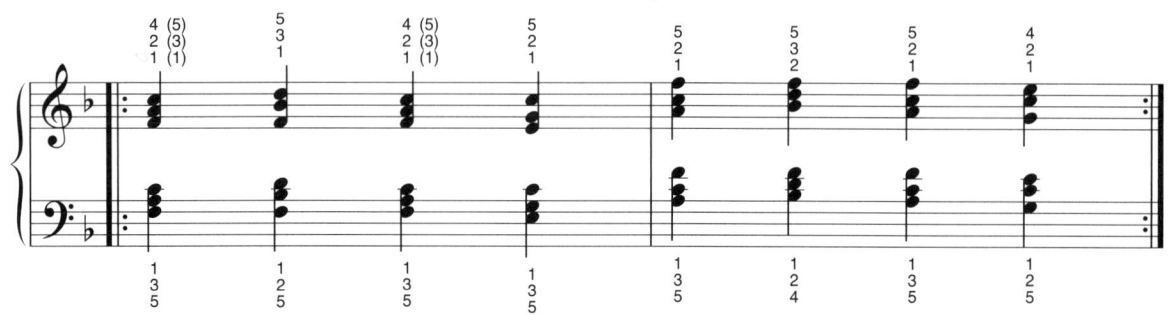

Technical Exercises

Group C: Riff | ♩=90

In the exam you will be asked to play the following riff to the backing track found on the BBK candidate book CD. The riff pattern shown in bars 1 and 2 should be played in the subsequent bars using the nearest right hand inversions for the stated chord. The chord relationship of I–IV should be followed throughout referring to the chord patterns in Group B above where necessary.

Technical Exercises

Grade 3

In this section, the examiner will ask you to play a selection of exercises drawn from each of the four groups shown below. Groups A, B & C contain examples of the kinds of scales and chords you can use when playing the pieces in the BBK Grade 3 candidate book. In Group D you will be asked to prepare the riff exercise and play it to the CD backing track. You do not need to memorise the exercises, and *while you cannot take this book into the exam* you can use the BBK Grade 3 candidate book. The examiner will be looking for a prompt and accurate response, fluency and consistency of pulse.

The examiner will give you the tempo in the exam. All scales and chords should be played using the piano patch.

Group A: Scales | Minor pentatonic scales | ♩=60

All scales are to be prepared hands separately and together.

1a. C minor pentatonic scale

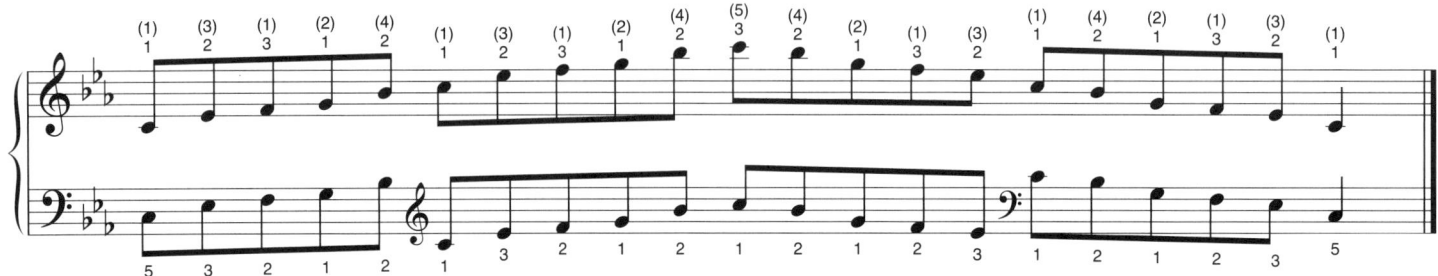

1b. G minor pentatonic scale

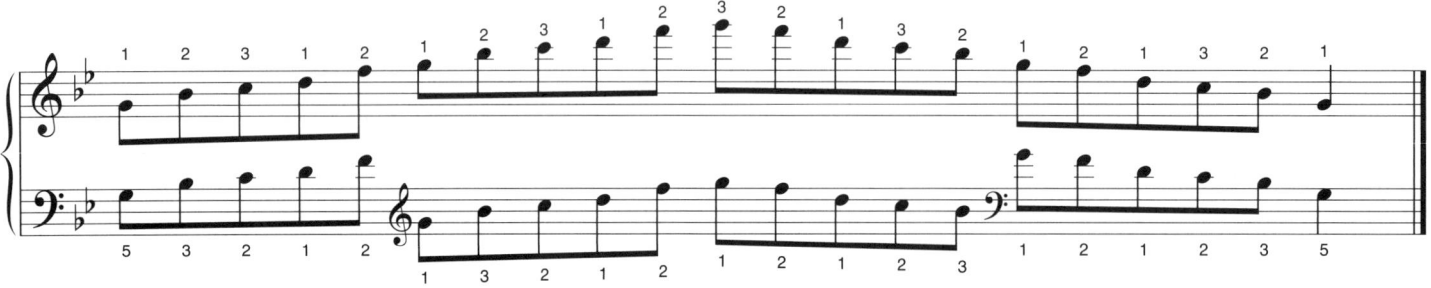

1c. F minor pentatonic scale

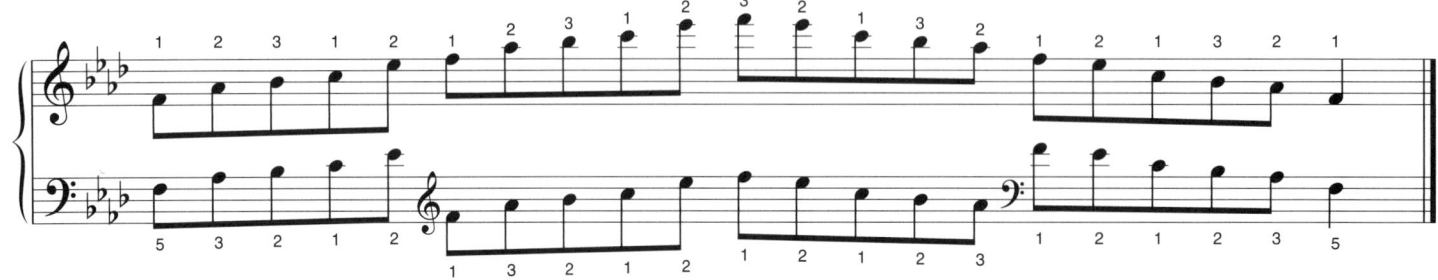

Technical Exercises

Group A: Scales | Natural minor scales | ♩=60

All scales are to be prepared hands separately and together.

2a. C natural minor scale

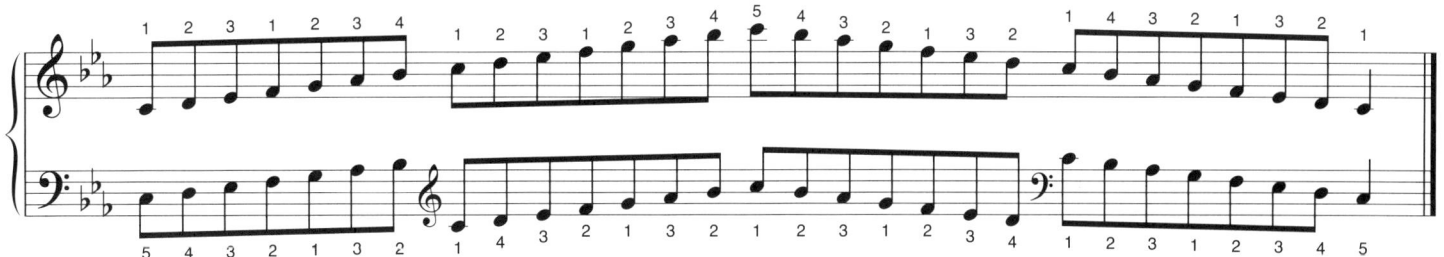

2b. G natural minor scale

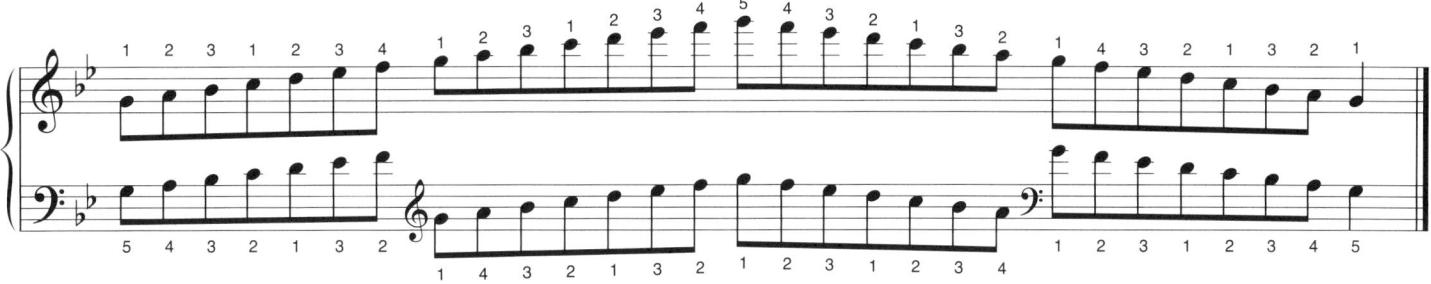

2c. F natural minor scale

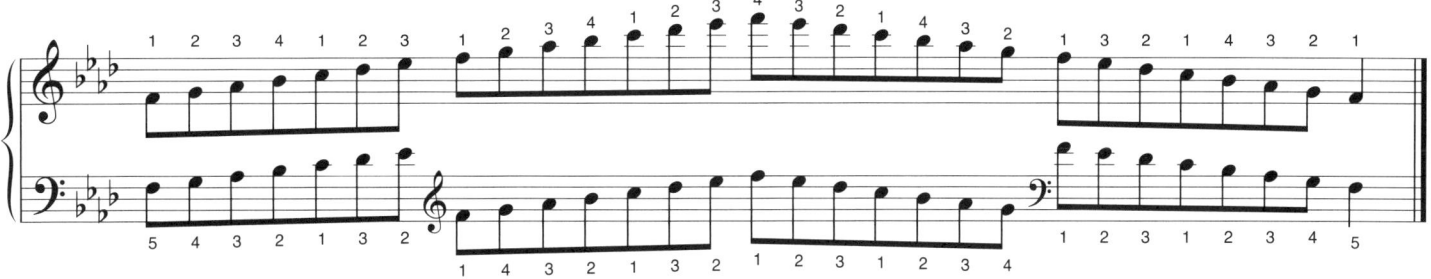

Technical Exercises

Group A: Scales | Major scales | ♩=60

All scales are to be prepared hands separately and together.

3a. D major scale

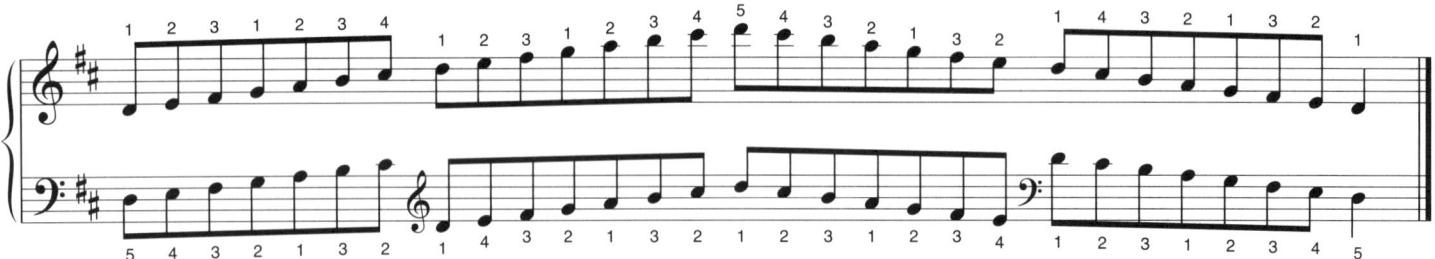

3b. A major scale

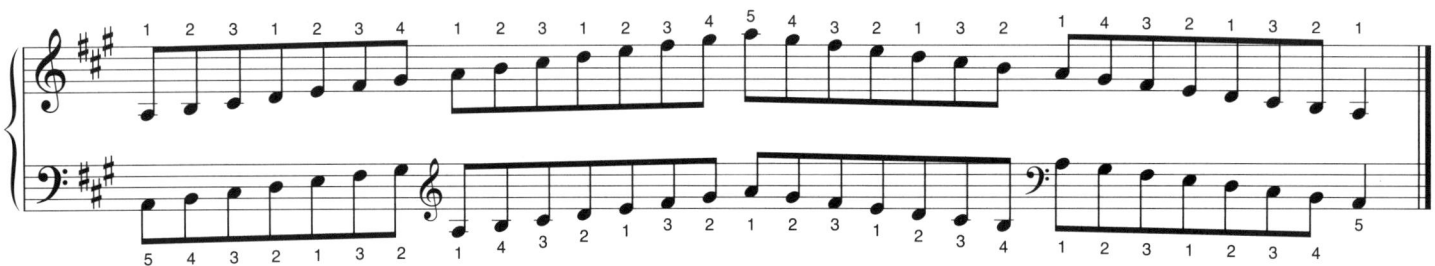

3c. B♭ major scale

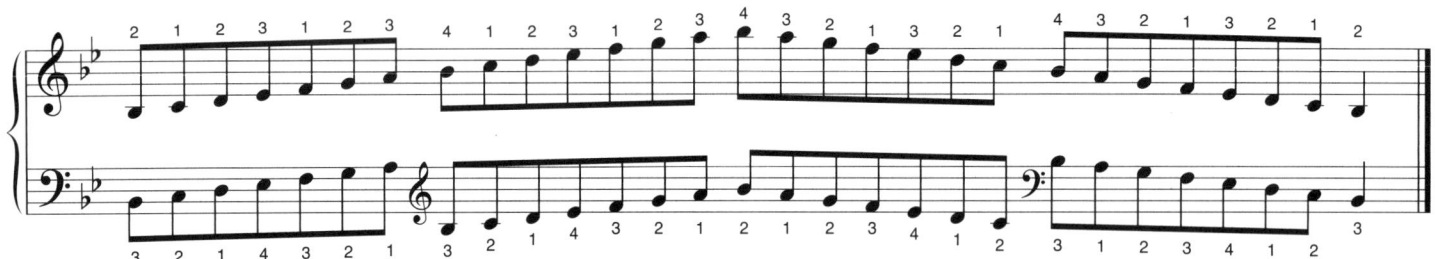

Technical Exercises

Group B: Chords | Chord sequence 1 | ♩=60

All chord sequences should be played with the right or left hand as directed by the examiner.

1a. Chord sequence in C minor

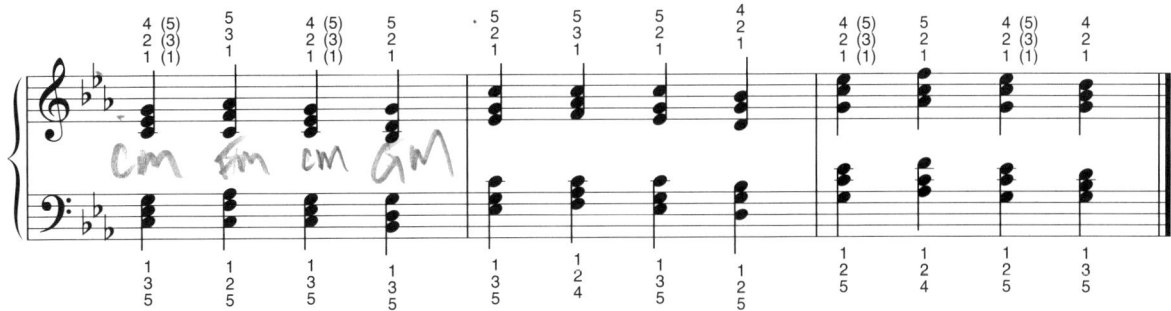

1b. Chord sequence in G minor

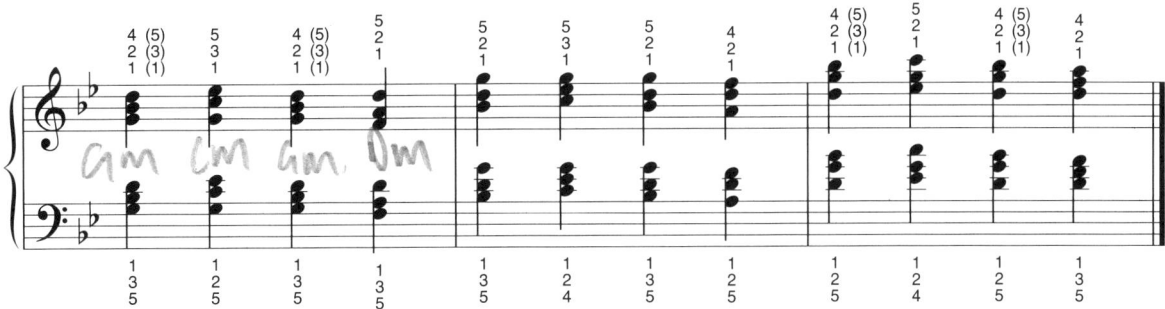

1c. Chord sequence in F minor

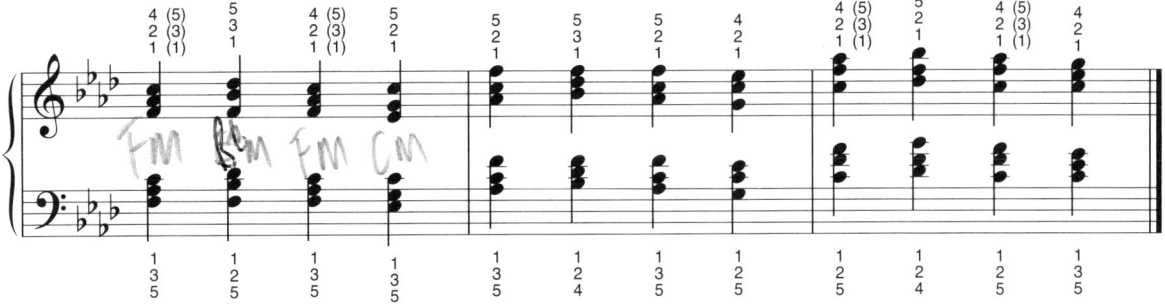

Technical Exercises

Group B: Chords | Chord sequence 2 | ♩=60

All chord sequences should be played with the right or left hand as directed by the examiner.

2a. Chord sequence in D major

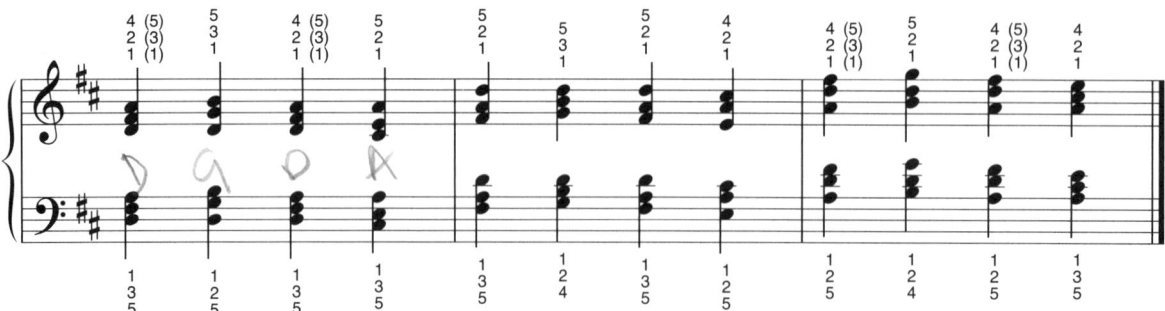

2b. Chord sequence in A major

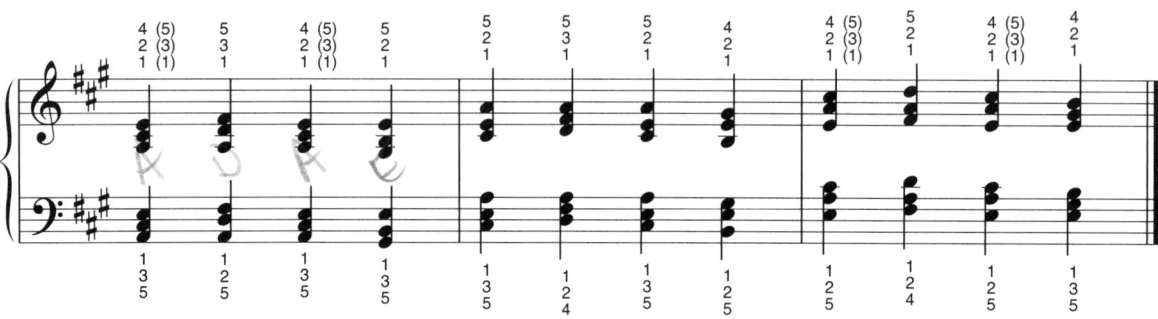

2c. Chord sequence in B♭ major

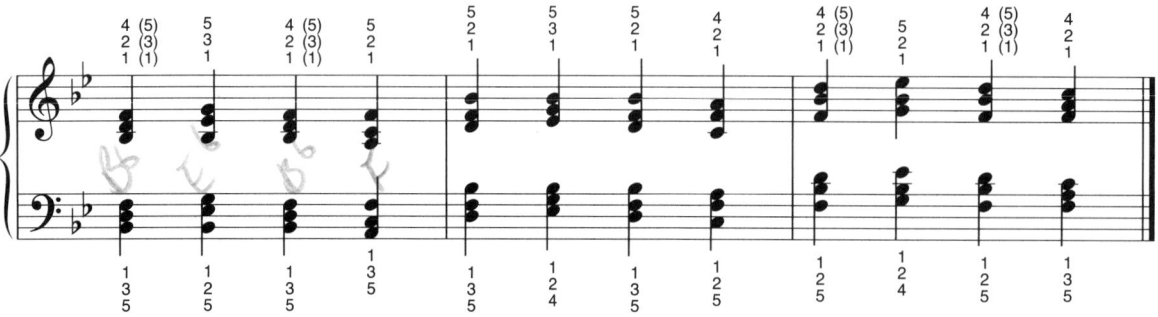

Technical Exercises

Group C: Dominant sevenths | ♩=60

1a. G⁷ exercise

1b. C⁷ exercise

1c. D⁷ exercise

1d. A⁷ exercise

1e. B♭⁷ exercise

Technical Exercises

Group D: Riff | ♩ = 120

In the exam you will be asked to play the following riff to the backing track found on the BBK candidate book CD. The riff shown in bars 1 & 2 should be played in the same shape in bars 3–12. The root note of the pattern to be played is shown in the music in each bar where the chord changes. Where only one bar is shown play only the first bar of the riff.

Technical Exercises

Grade 4

In this section, the examiner will ask you to play a selection of exercises drawn from each of the four groups shown below. Groups A, B & C contain examples of the kinds of scales and chords you can use when playing the pieces in the BBK Grade 4 candidate book. In Group D you will be asked to prepare the riff exercise and play it to the CD backing track. You do not need to memorise the exercises, and *while you cannot take this book into the exam* you can use the BBK Grade 4 candidate book. The examiner will be looking for a prompt and accurate response, fluency and consistency of pulse.

The examiner will give you the tempo in the exam. All scales and chords should be played using the piano patch.

Candidates can choose to play groups A, B & C as follows:
    either *Group A:* C, D♭ (C♯), D **and** *Groups B & C:* E♭, E, F
    or *Group A:* E♭, E, F **and** *Groups B & C:* C, D♭ (C♯), D

Group A: Scales | Blues scales | ♩=100

All scales are to be prepared hands separately and together.

1a. C blues scale

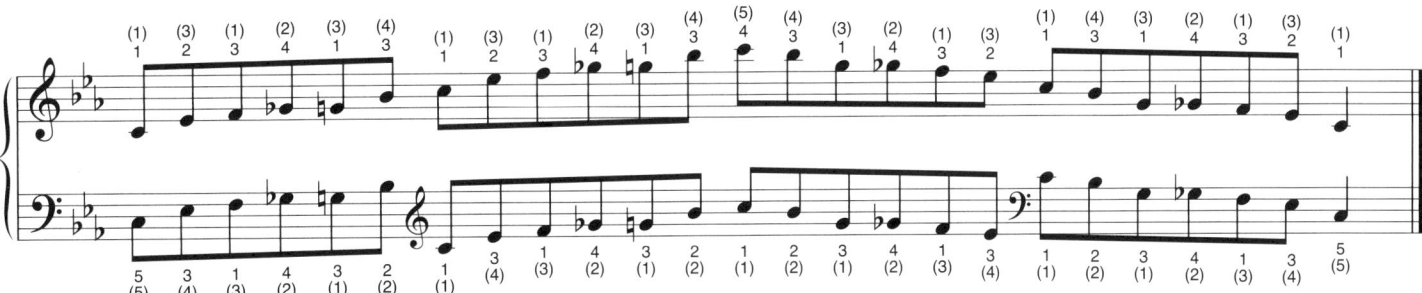

1b. C♯ blues scale

1c. D blues scale

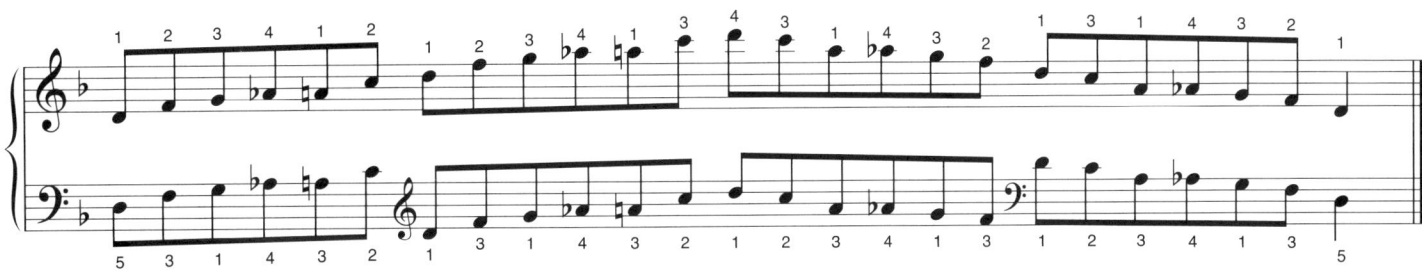

Technical Exercises

1d. E♭ blues scale

1e. E blues scale

1f. F blues scale

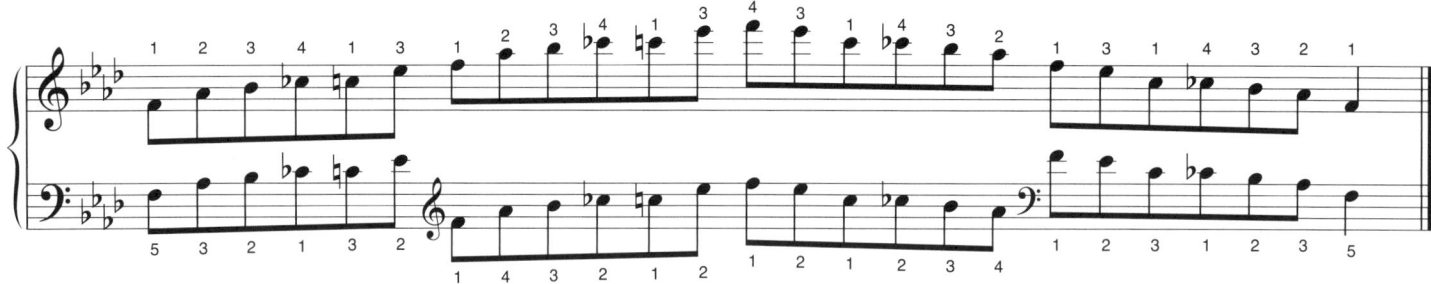

Group A: Scales | Natural minor scales | ♩=100

All scales are to be prepared hands separately and together.

2a. C natural minor scale

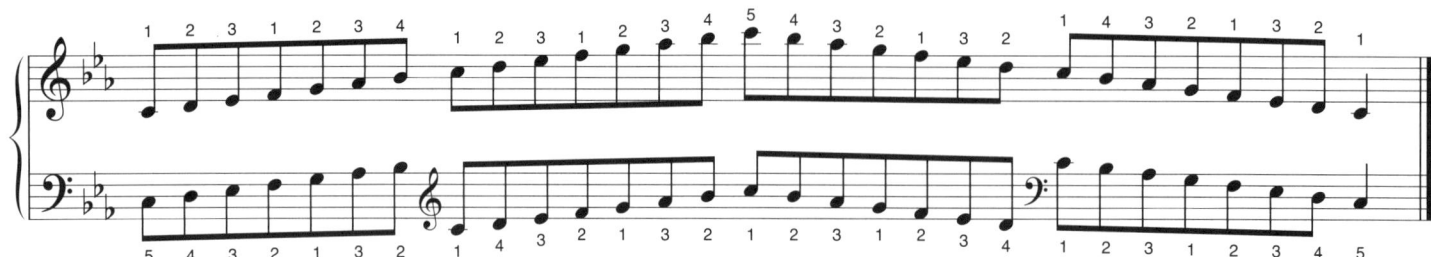

2b. C♯ natural minor scale

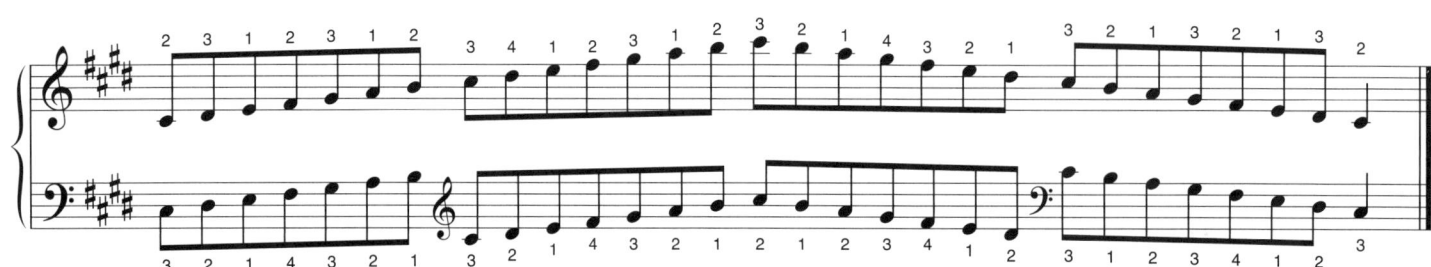

Technical Exercises

2c. D natural minor scale

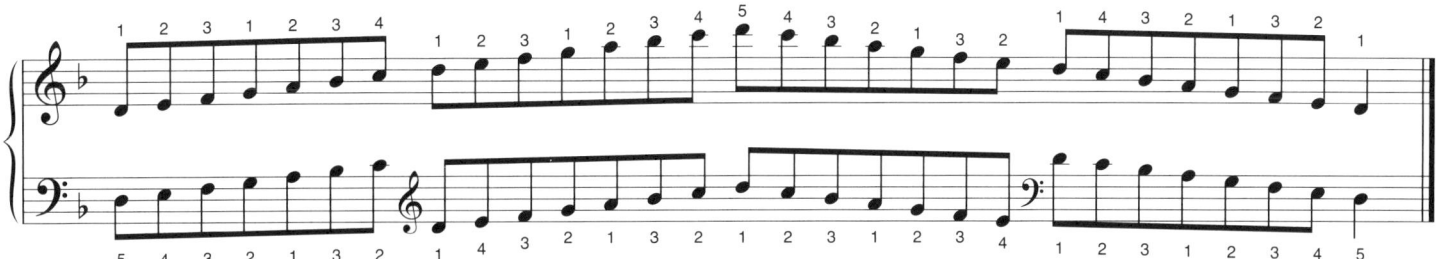

2d. E♭ natural minor scale

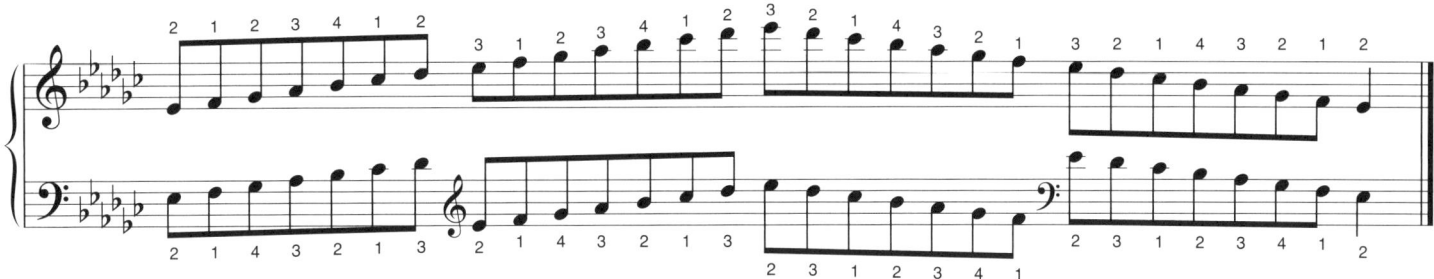

2e. E natural minor scale

2f. F natural minor scale

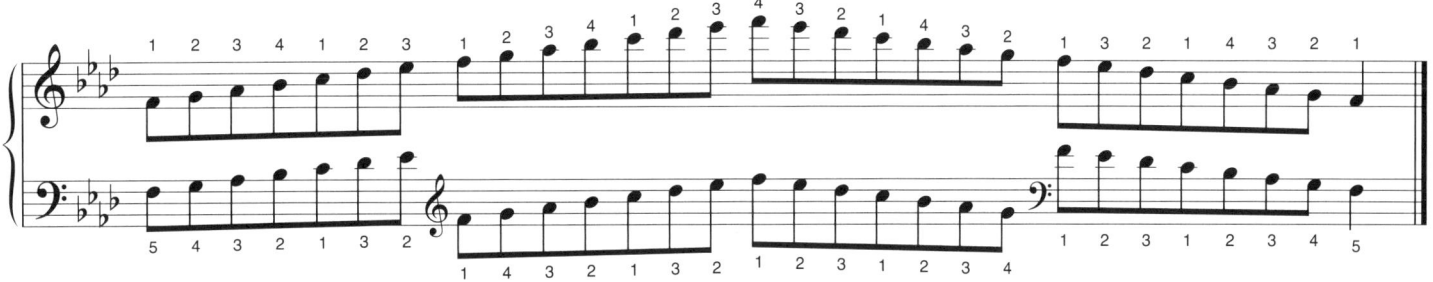

Group A: Scales | Major scales | ♩=100

All scales are to be prepared hands separately and together.

3a. C major scale

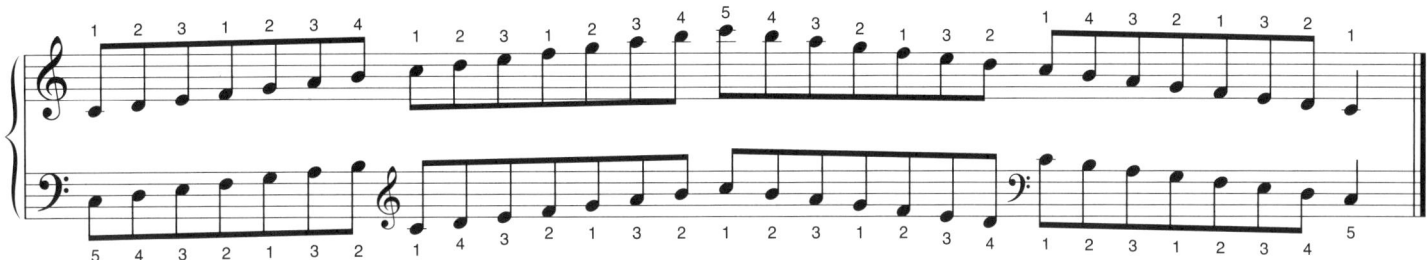

Technical Exercises

3b. D♭ major scale

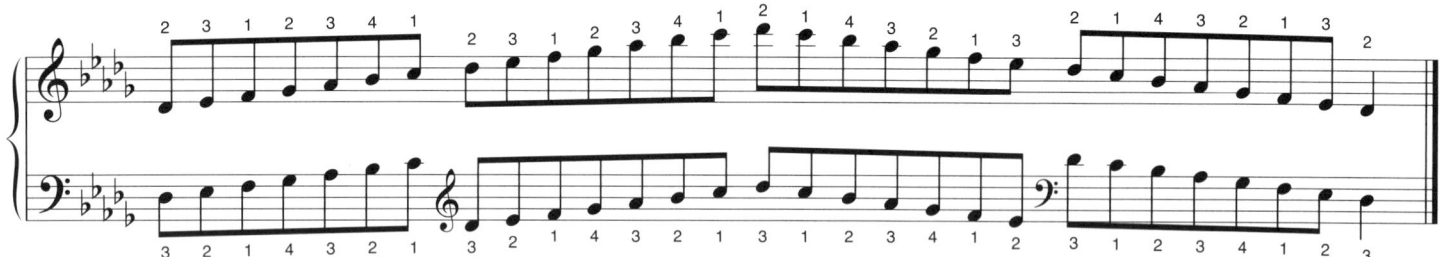

3c. D major scale

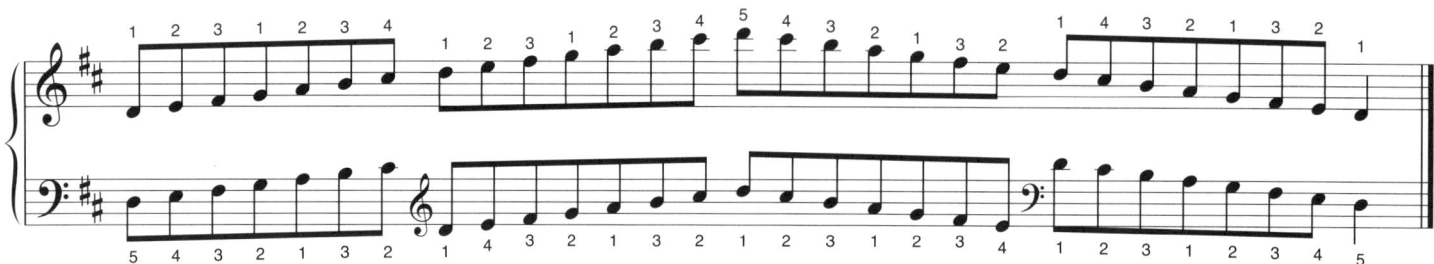

3d. E♭ major scale

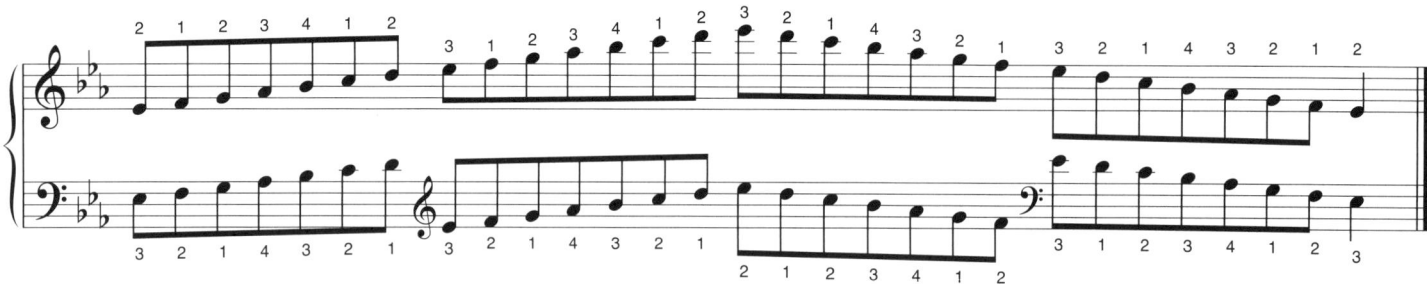

3e. E major scale

3f. F major scale

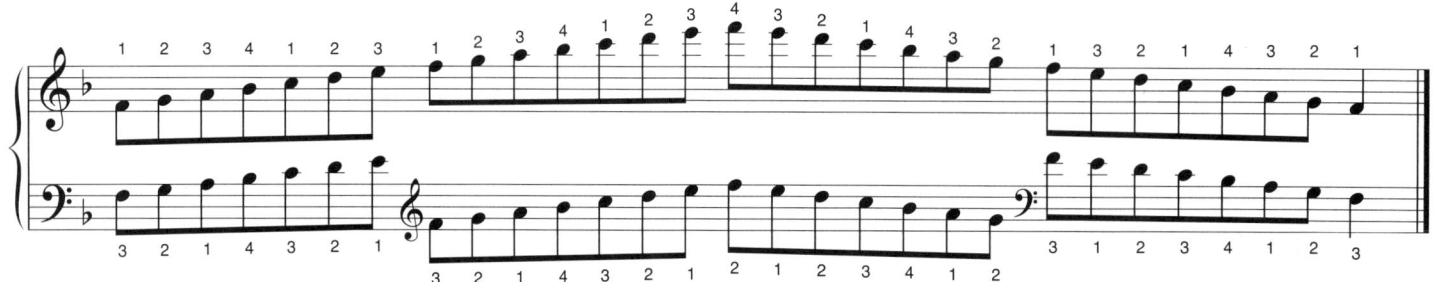

Technical Exercises

Group A: Scales | Mixolydian mode | ♩=100

All scales are to be prepared hands separately and together.

4a. C mixolydian mode

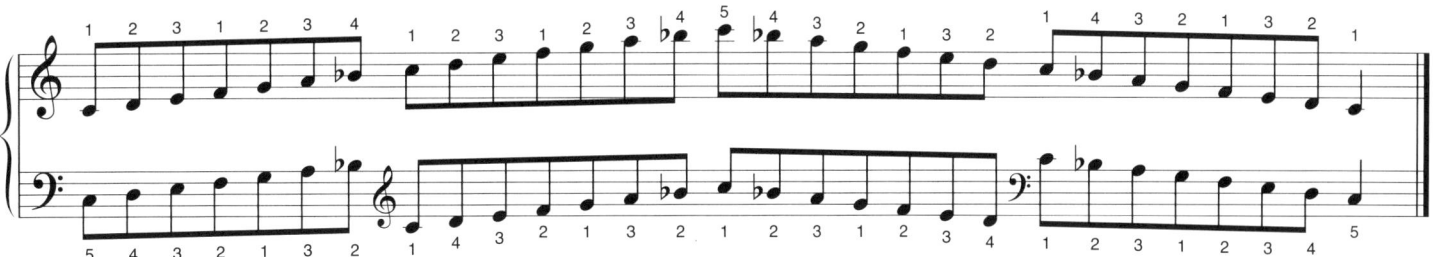

4b. D♭ mixolydian mode

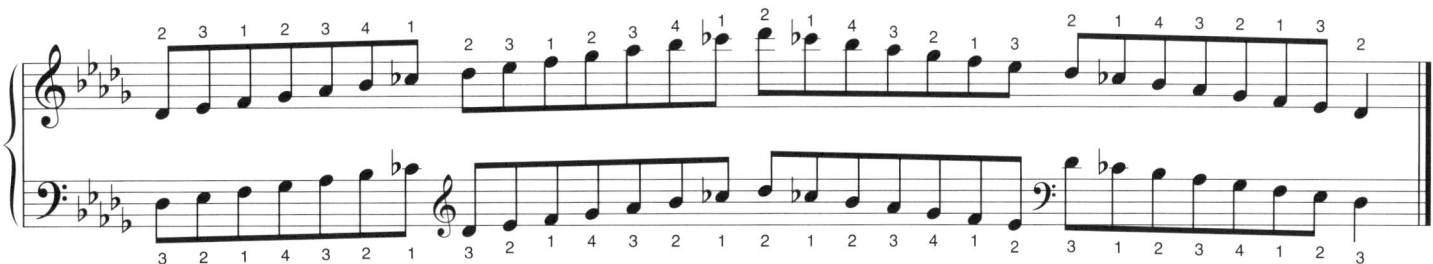

4c. D mixolydian mode

4d. E♭ mixolydian mode

4e. E mixolydian mode

Technical Exercises

4f. F mixolydian mode

Group B: Chords | Key of C minor | ♩=100

You must prepare the following minor chord sequences with both right and left hands separately. The examiner will select two consecutive chord sequences for you to play: e.g. 1 & 2 or 2 & 3.

1.

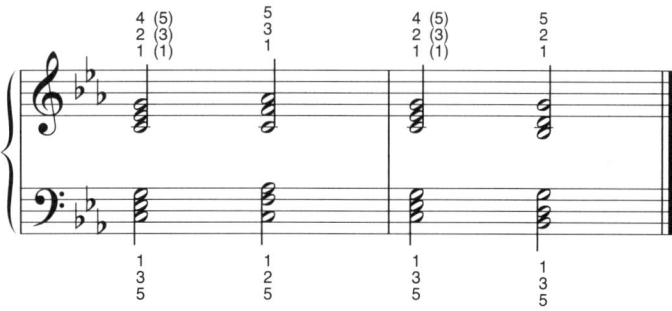

2.

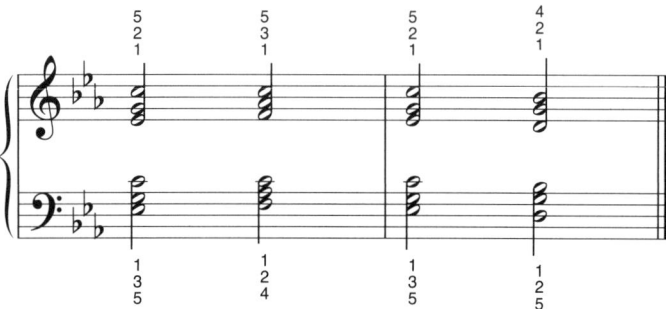

3.

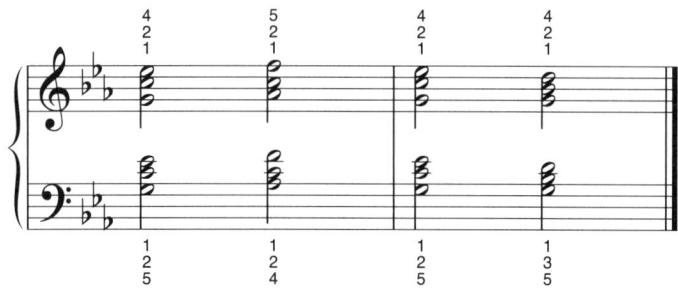

Technical Exercises

Group B: Chords | Key of C♯ minor | ♩=100

You must prepare the following minor chord sequences with both right and left hands separately. The examiner will select two consecutive chord sequences for you to play: e.g. 1 & 2 or 2 & 3.

1.

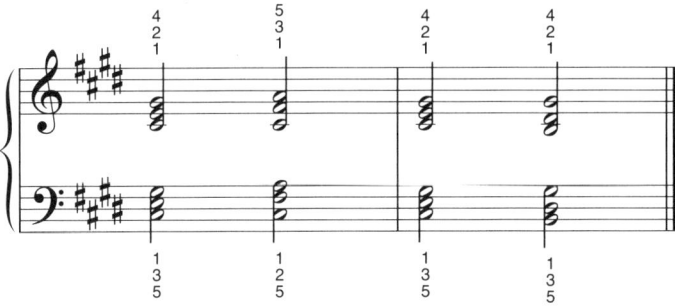

2.

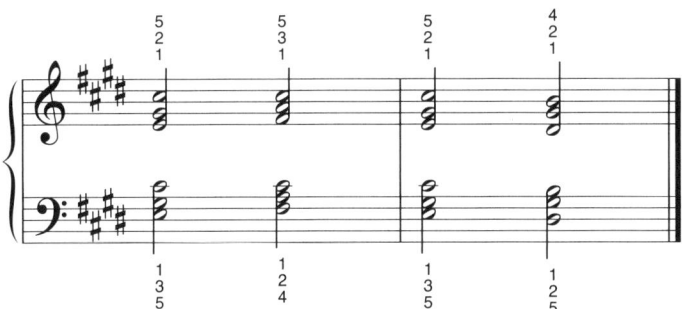

3.

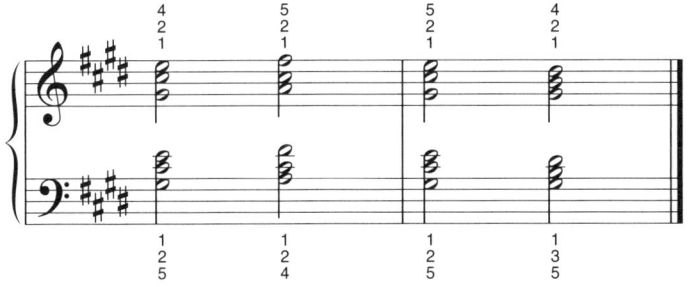

Technical Exercises

Group B: Chords | Key of D minor | ♩=100

You must prepare the following minor chord sequences with both right and left hands separately. The examiner will select two consecutive chord sequences for you to play: e.g. 1 & 2 or 2 & 3.

1.

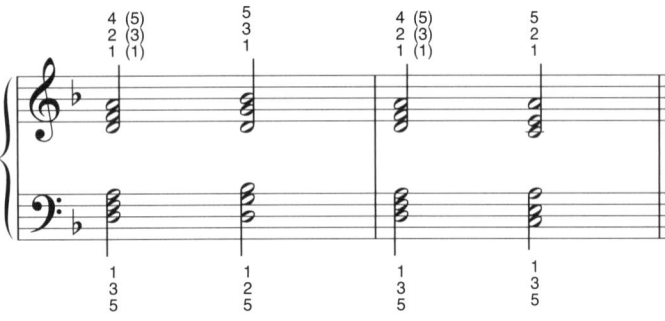

2.

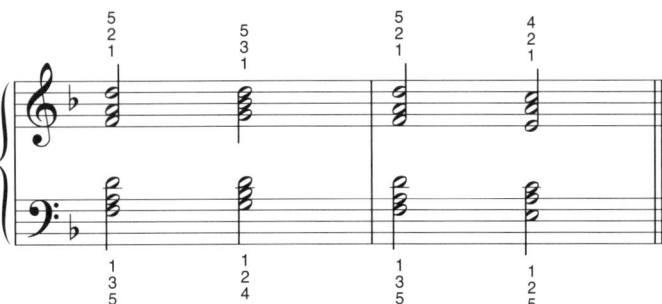

3.

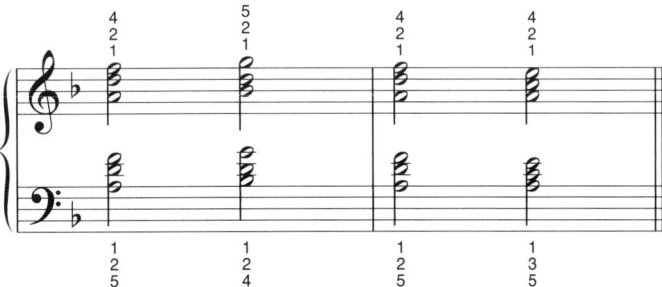

Technical Exercises

Group B: Chords | Key of E♭ minor | ♩=100

You must prepare the following minor chord sequences with both right and left hands separately. The examiner will select two consecutive chord sequences for you to play: e.g. 1 & 2 or 2 & 3.

1.

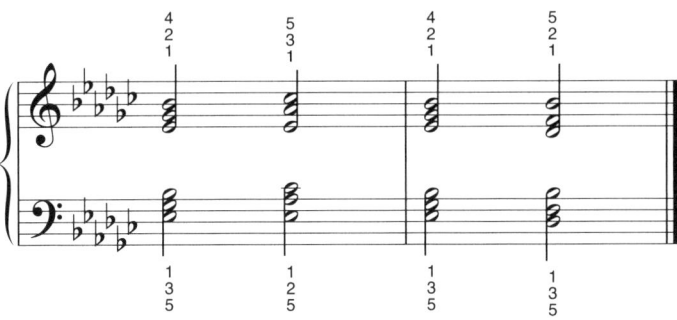

2.

3.

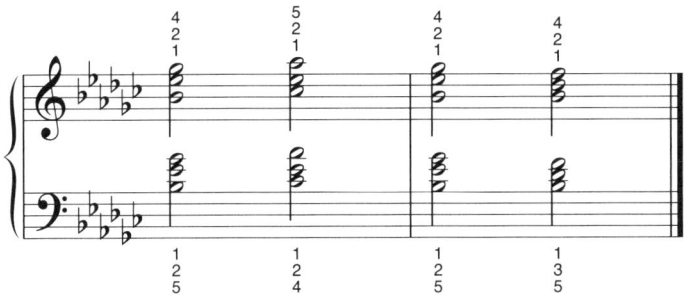

Technical Exercises

Group B: Chords | Key of E minor | ♩=100

You must prepare the following minor chord sequences with both right and left hands separately. The examiner will select two consecutive chord sequences for you to play: e.g. 1 & 2 or 2 & 3.

1.

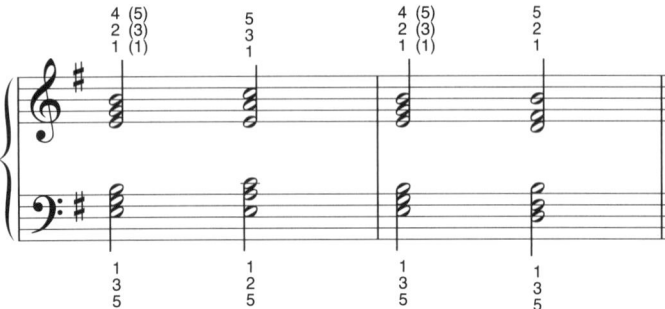

2.

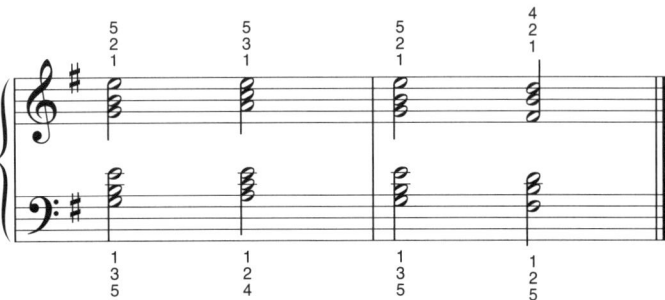

3.

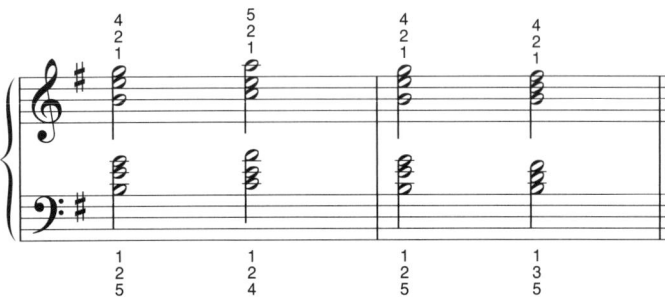

Technical Exercises

Group B: Chords | Key of F minor | ♩=100

You must prepare the following minor chord sequences with both right and left hands separately. The examiner will select two consecutive chord sequences for you to play: e.g. 1 & 2 or 2 & 3.

1.

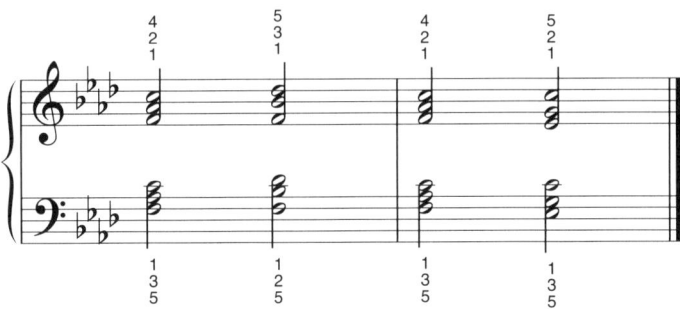

2.

3.

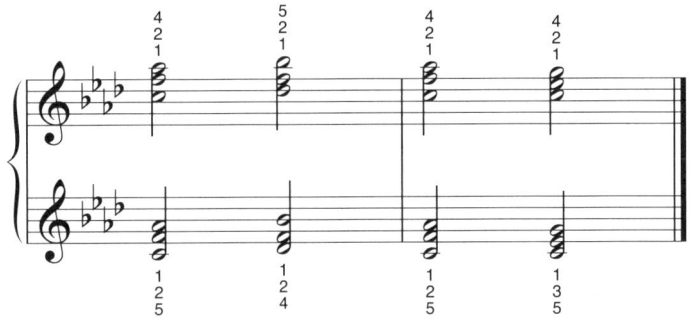

Technical Exercises

Group B: Chords | Key of C major | ♩=100

You must prepare the following major chord sequences with both right and left hands separately. The examiner will select two consecutive chord sequences for you to play: e.g. 1 & 2 or 2 & 3.

1.

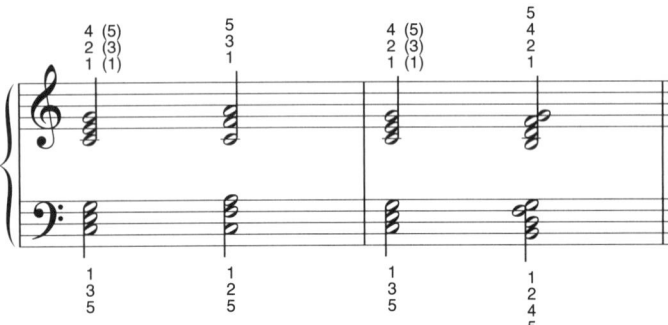

2.

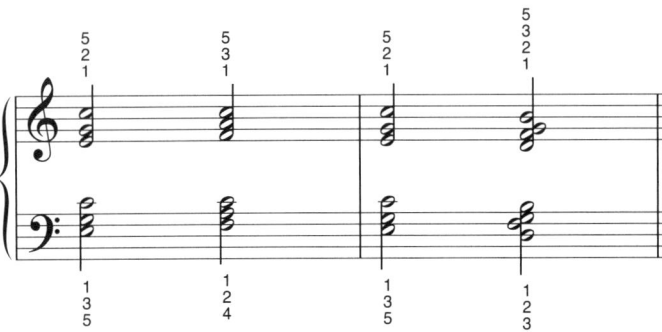

3.

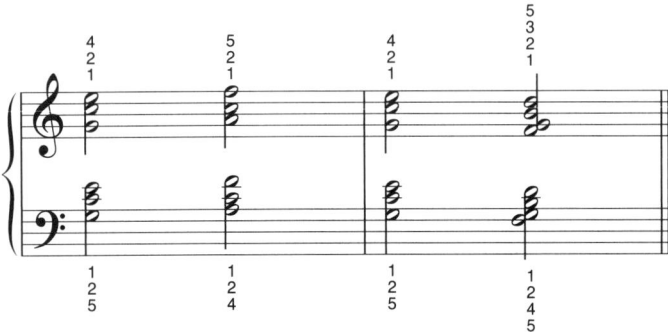

Technical Exercises

Group B: Chords | Key of D♭ major | ♩=100

You must prepare the following major chord sequences with both right and left hands separately. The examiner will select two consecutive chord sequences for you to play: e.g. 1 & 2 or 2 & 3.

1.

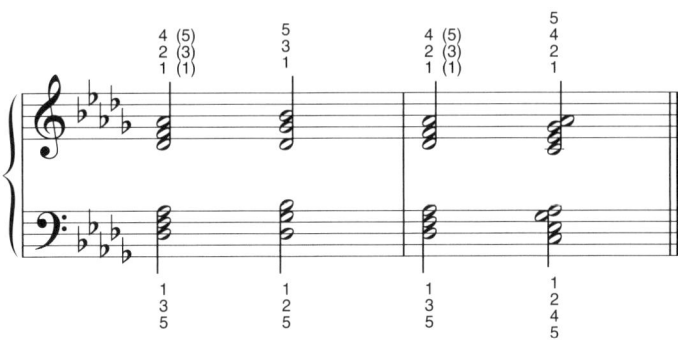

2.

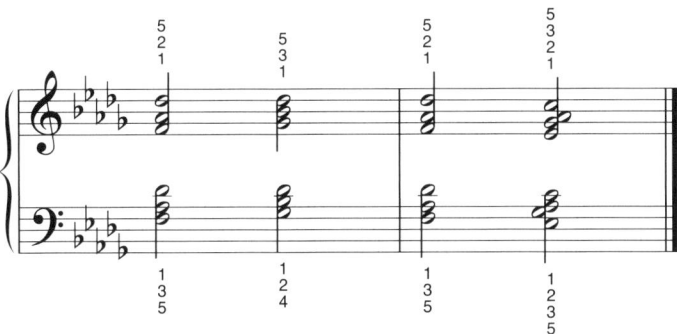

3.

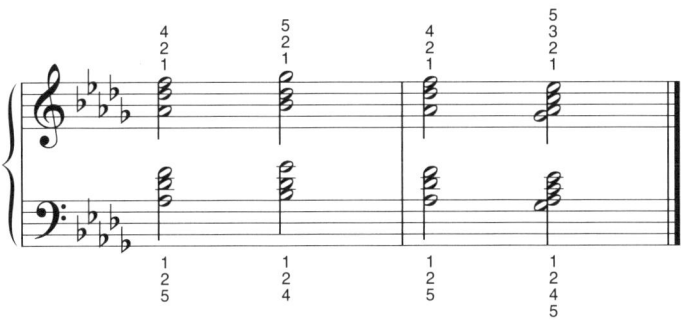

Technical Exercises

Group B: Chords | Key of D major | ♩=100

You must prepare the following major chord sequences with both right and left hands separately. The examiner will select two consecutive chord sequences for you to play: e.g. 1 & 2 or 2 & 3.

1.

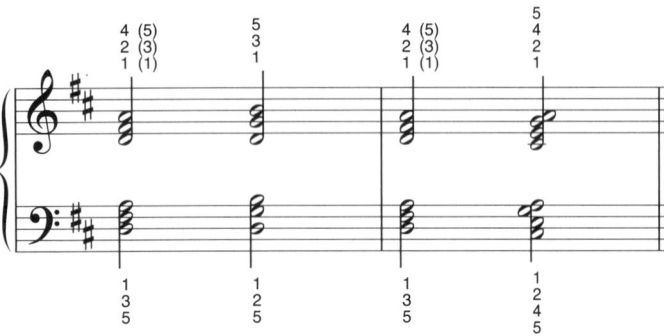

2.

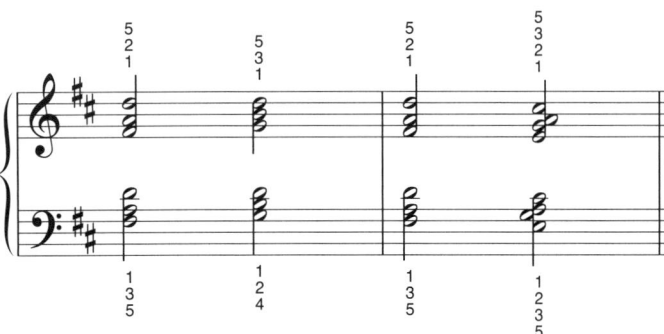

3.

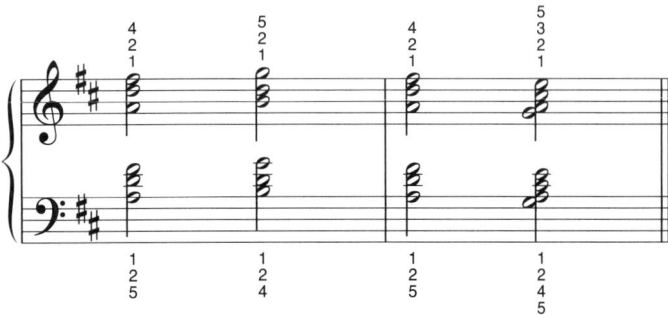

Technical Exercises

Group B: Chords | Key of E♭ major | ♩=100

You must prepare the following major chord sequences with both right and left hands separately. The examiner will select two consecutive chord sequences for you to play: e.g. 1 & 2 or 2 & 3.

1.

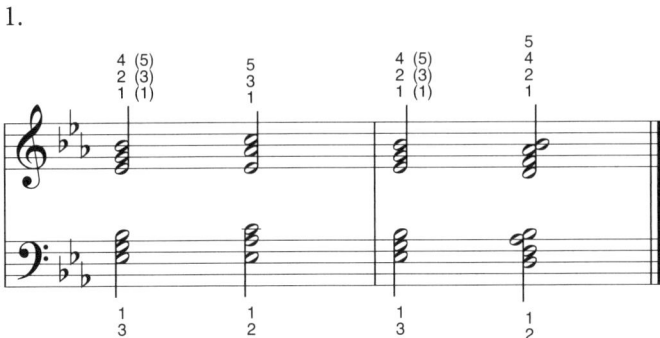

2.

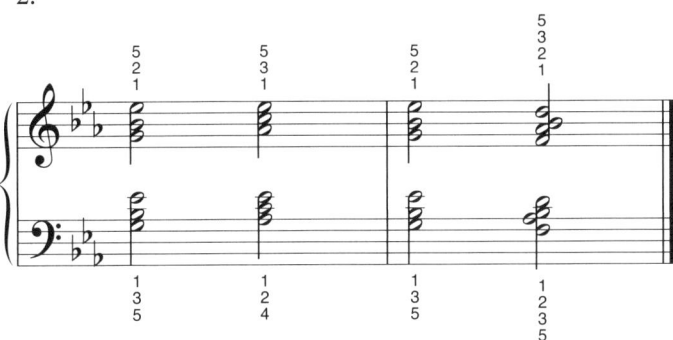

3.

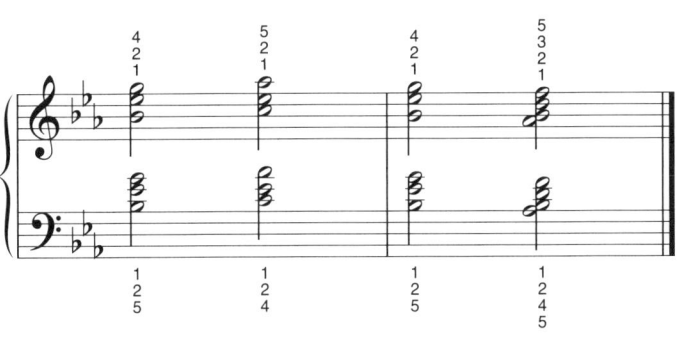

Technical Exercises

Group B: Chords | Key of E major | ♩=100

You must prepare the following major chord sequences with both right and left hands separately. The examiner will select two consecutive chord sequences for you to play: e.g. 1 & 2 or 2 & 3.

1.

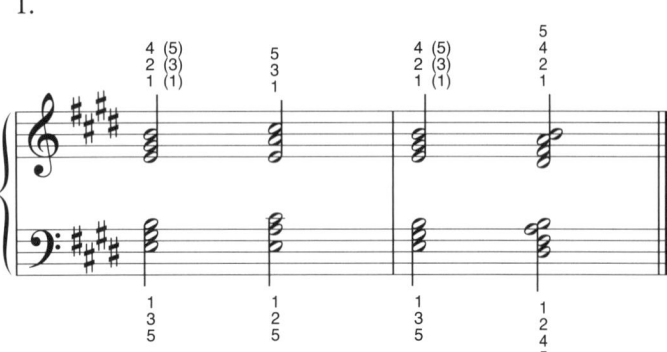

2.

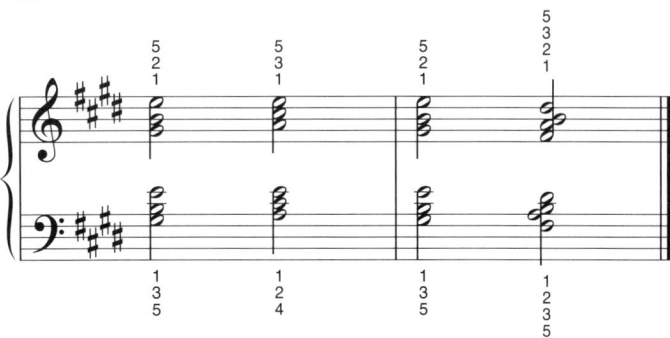

3.

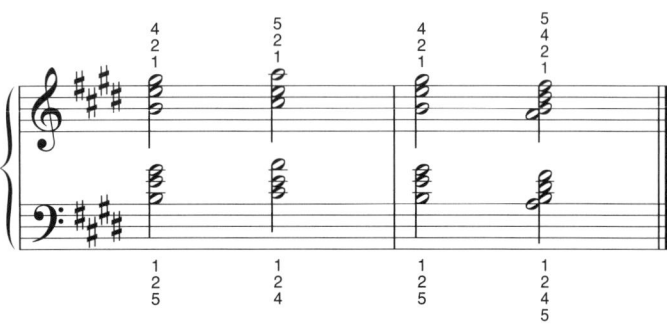

Technical Exercises

Group B: Chords | Key of F major | ♩=100

You must prepare the following major chord sequences with both right and left hands separately. The examiner will select two consecutive chord sequences for you to play: e.g. 1 & 2 or 2 & 3.

1.

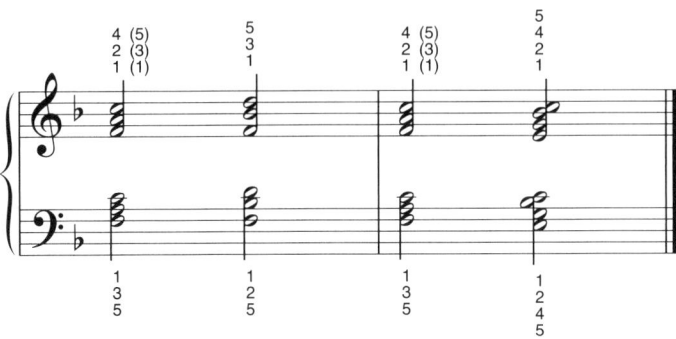

2.

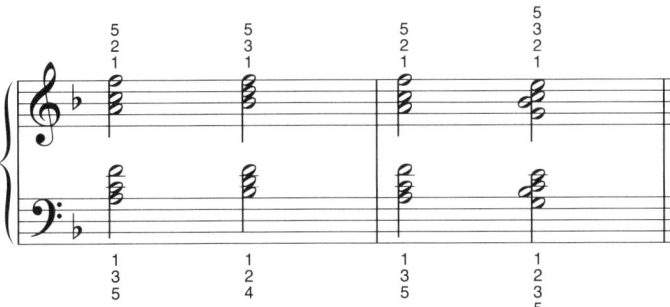

3.

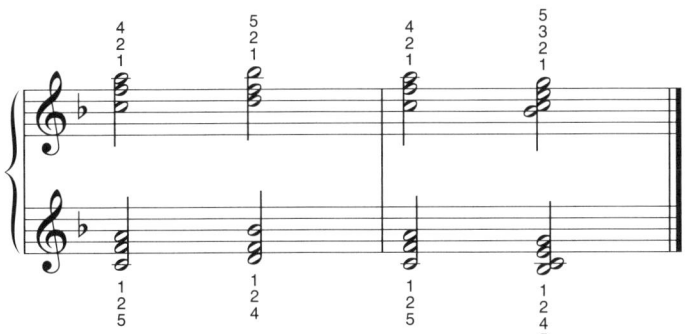

Technical Exercises

Group C: Minor sevenths | ♩=100

1a. C minor⁷ exercise

1b. C♯ minor⁷ exercise

1c. D minor⁷ exercise

1d. E♭ minor⁷ exercise

1e. E minor⁷ exercise

Technical Exercises

1f. F minor ^{7} exercise

Group D: Riff | ♩=135

In the exam you will be asked to play the following riff to the backing track found on the BBK candidate book CD. The riff shown in bar 1 should be played in the same shape in the bars 2–8. The root note of the pattern to be played is shown in the music in each bar where the chord changes. Where only one bar is shown play only the first bar of the riff.

Funk
Patch: Electric Piano

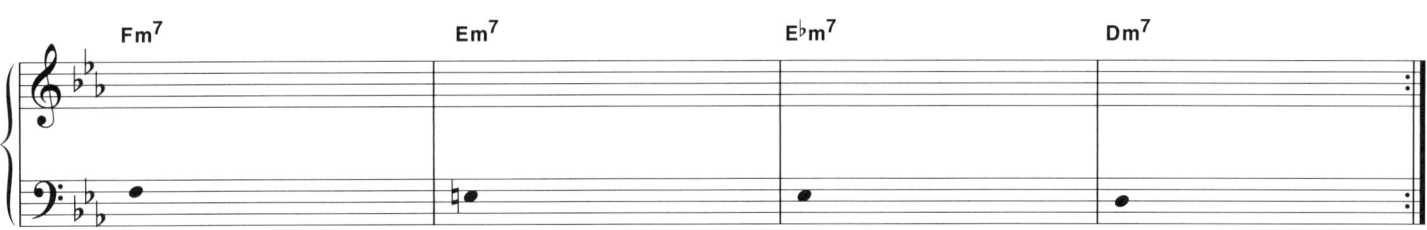

Technical Exercises

Grade 5

In this section, the examiner will ask you to play a selection of exercises drawn from each of the four groups shown below. Groups A, B & C contain examples of the kinds of scales and chords you can use when playing the pieces in the BBK Grade 5 candidate book. In Group D you will be asked to prepare the riff exercise and play it to the CD backing track found on the candidate book CD. You do not need to memorise the exercises, and *while you cannot take this book into the exam* you can use the BBK Grade 5 candidate book. The examiner will be looking for a prompt and accurate response, fluency and consistency of pulse.

The examiner will give you the tempo in the exam. All scales and chords should be played using the piano patch.

Candidates can choose to play groups A, B & C as follows:
- **either** *Group A:* F♯, G, A♭ **and** *Groups B & C:* A, B♭, B
- **or** *Group A:* A, B♭, B **and** *Groups B & C:* F♯, G, A♭

Group A: Scales | Blues scales | ♩ = 100

All scales are to be prepared hands separately and together.

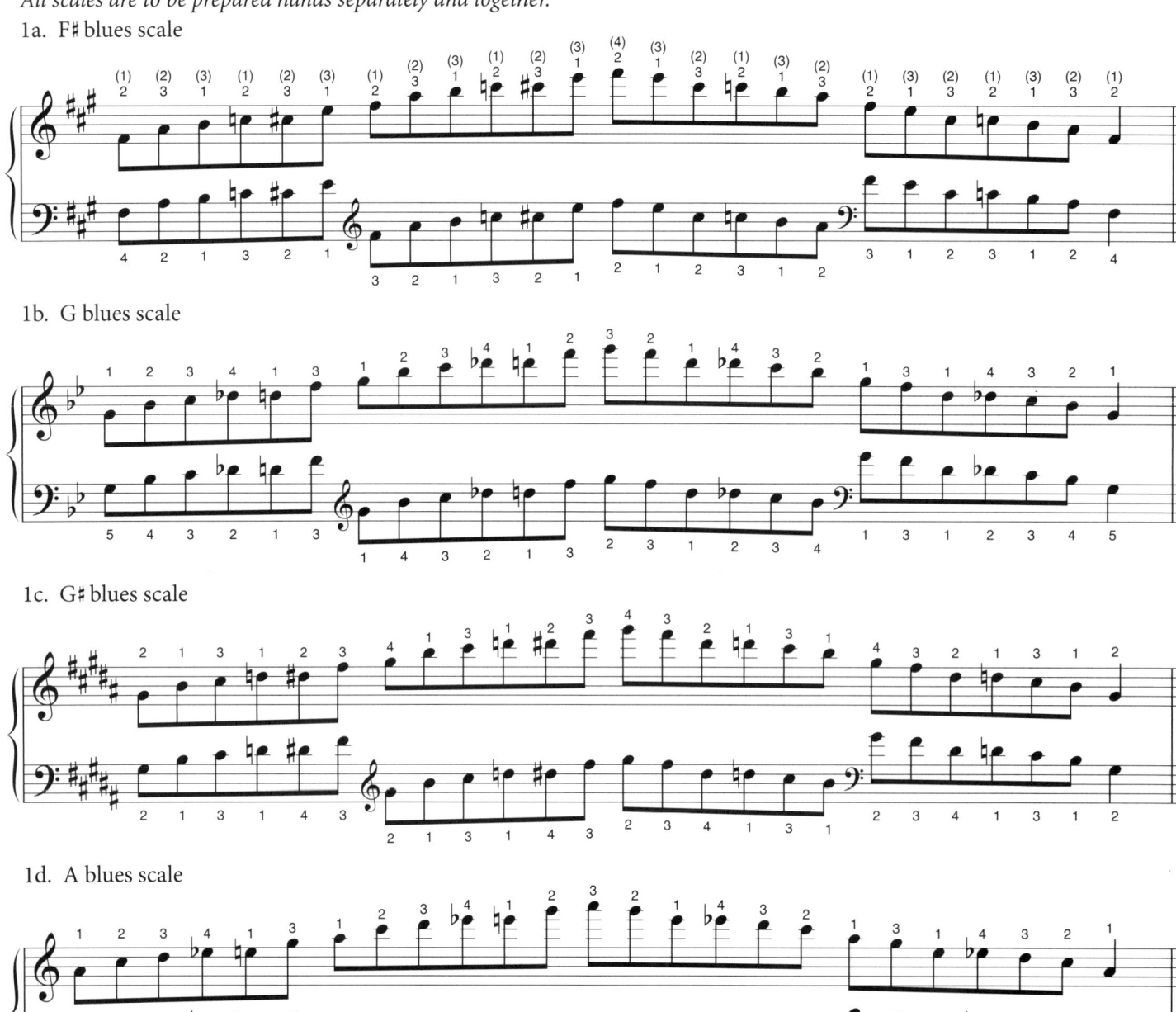

1a. F♯ blues scale

1b. G blues scale

1c. G♯ blues scale

1d. A blues scale

Technical Exercises

1e. B♭ blues scale

1f. B blues scale

Group A: Scales | Natural minor scales | ♩=100

All scales are to be prepared hands separately and together.

2a. F♯ natural minor scale

2b. G natural minor scale

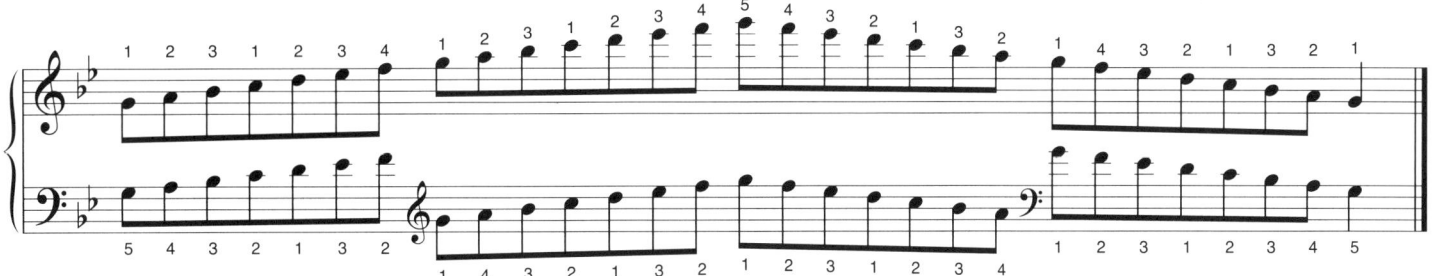

2c. G♯ natural minor scale

Technical Exercises

2d. A natural minor scale

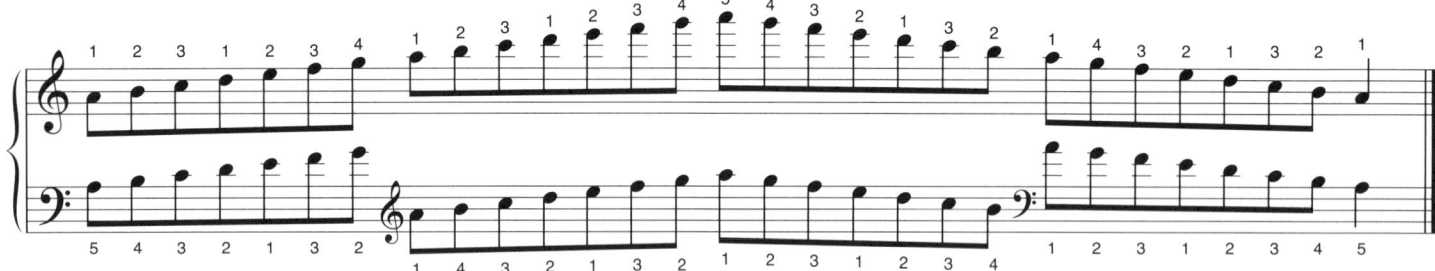

2e. B♭ natural minor scale

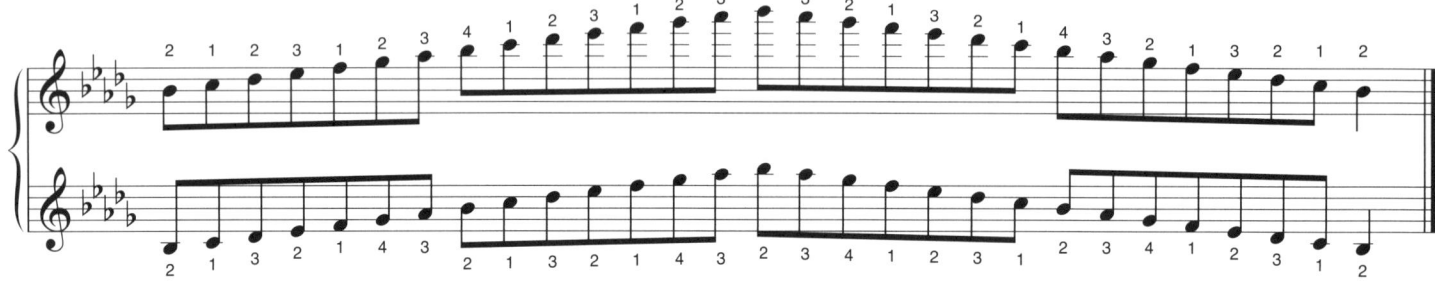

2f. B natural minor scale

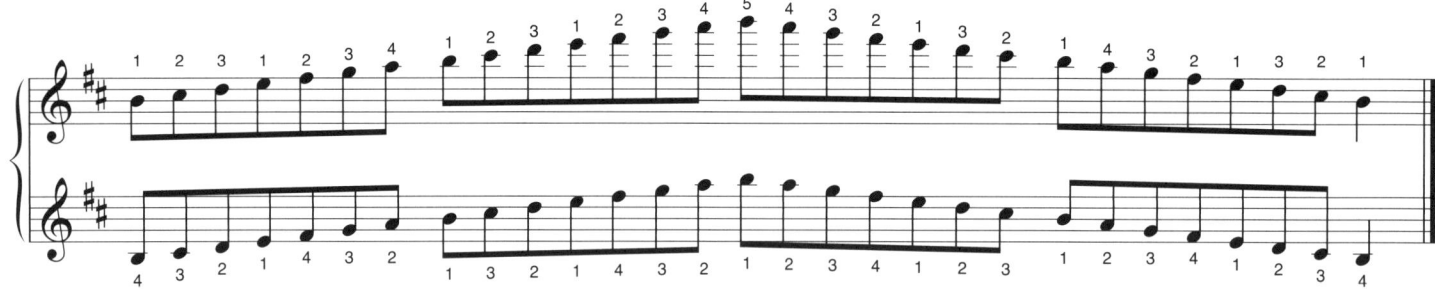

Group A: Scales | Major scales | ♩=100

All scales are to be prepared hands separately and together.

3a. F♯ major scale

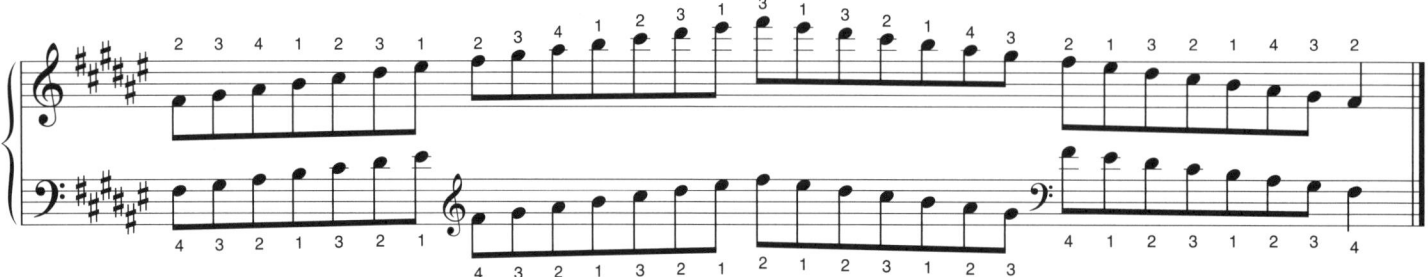

3b. G major scale

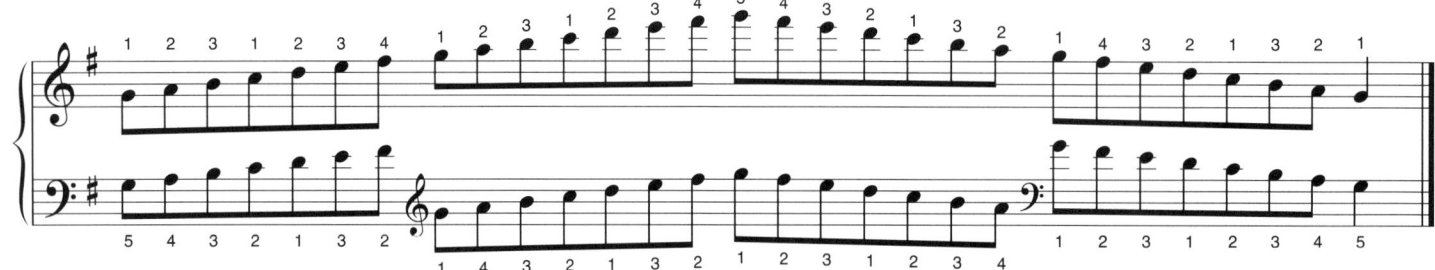

Technical Exercises

3c. A♭ major scale

3d. A major scale

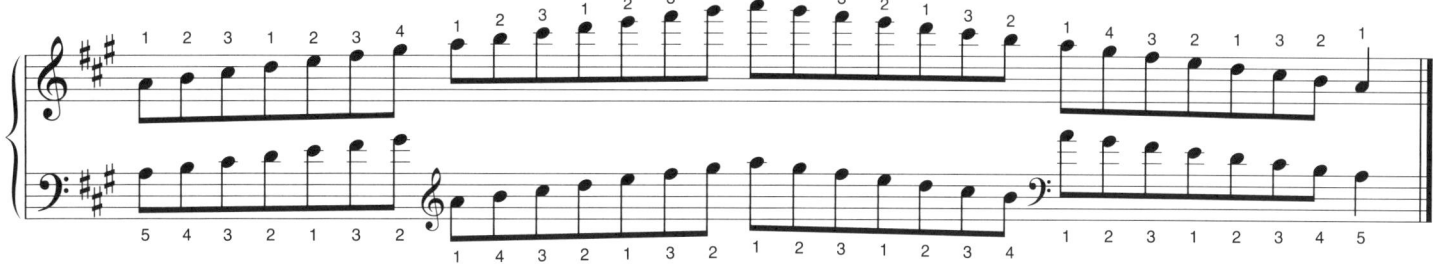

3e. B♭ major scale

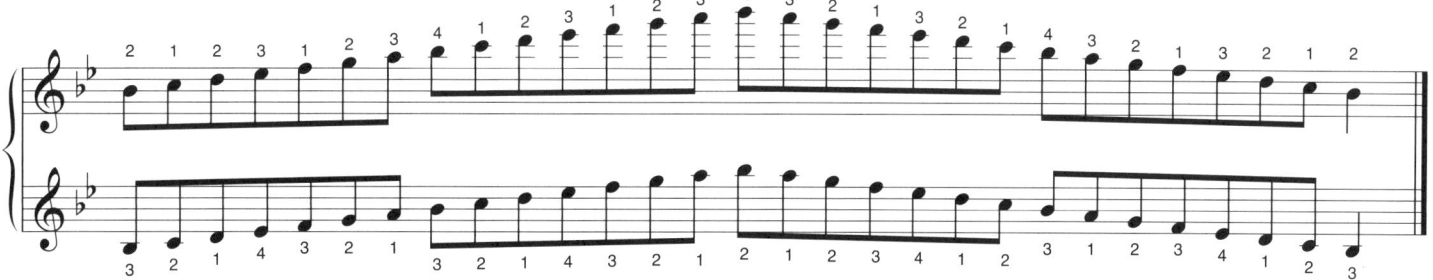

3f. B major scale

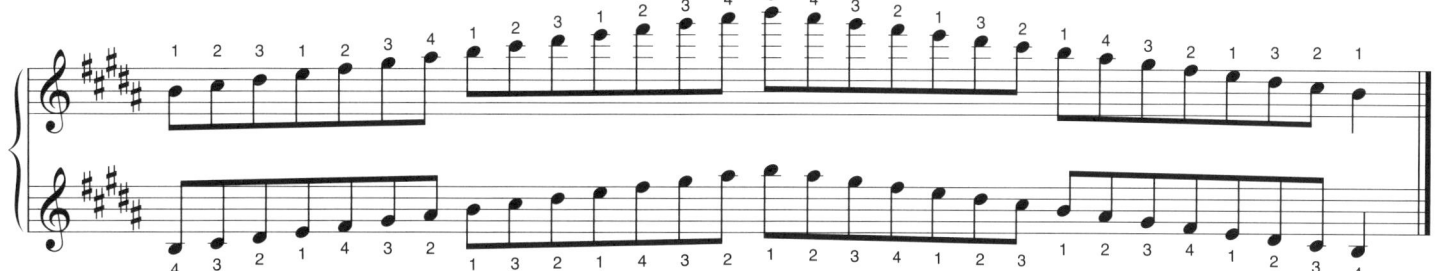

Group A: Scales | Mixolydian mode | ♩=100

All scales are to be prepared hands separately and together.

4a. F♯ mixolydian mode

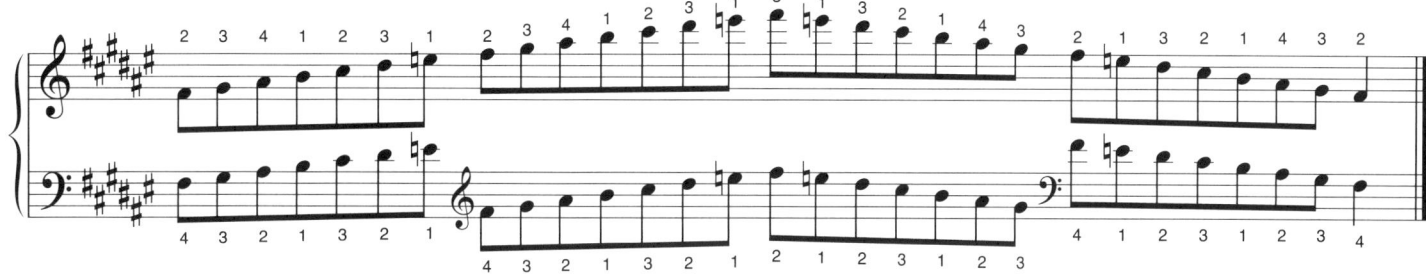

Technical Exercises

4b. G mixolydian mode

4c. A♭ mixolydian mode

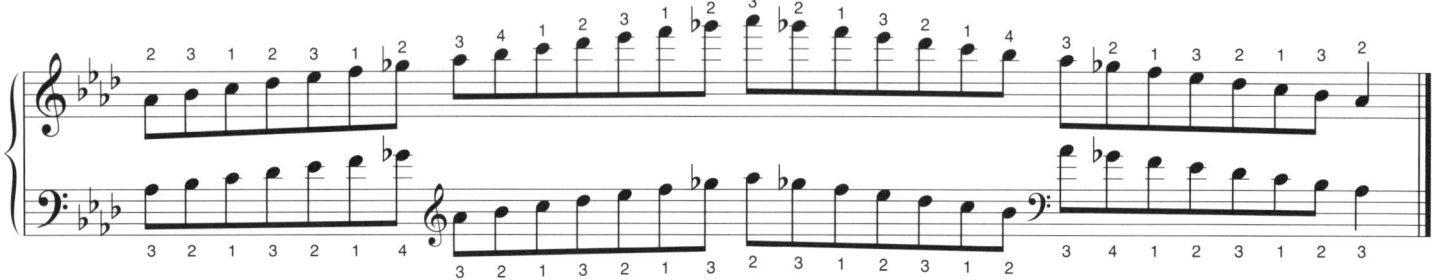

4d. A mixolydian mode

4e. B♭ mixolydian mode

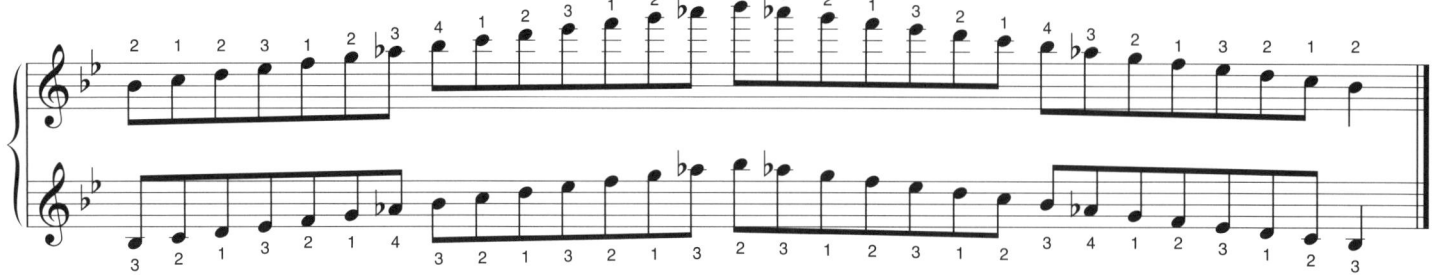

4f. B mixolydian mode

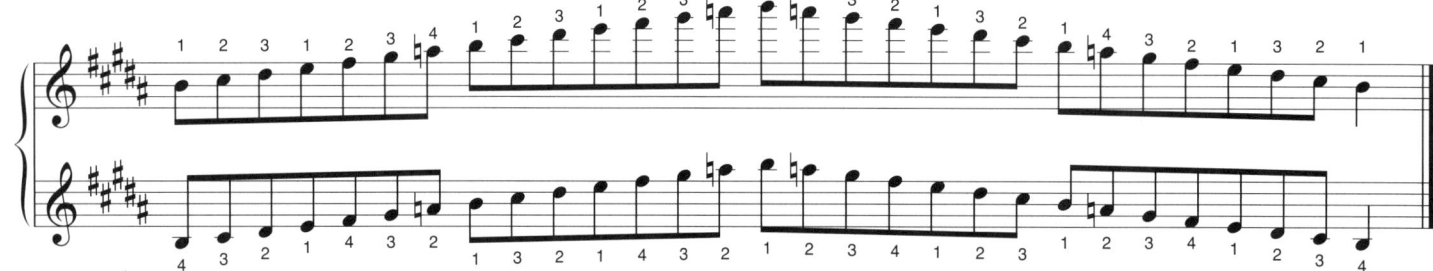

Technical Exercises

Group B: Chords | Key of F♯ major | ♩=100

You must prepare the following major chord sequences with both right and left hands separately. The examiner will select two consecutive chord sequences for you to play: e.g. 1 & 2, 2 & 3 or 3 & 4.

1.

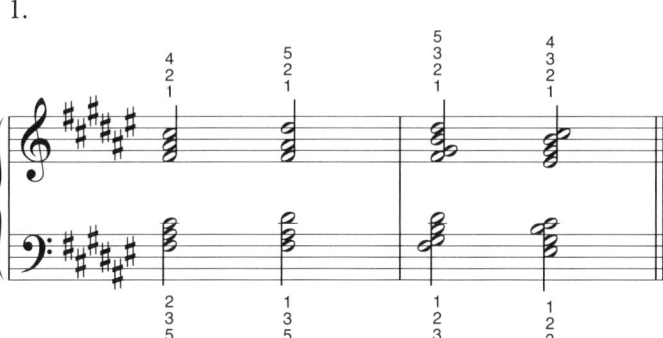

2.

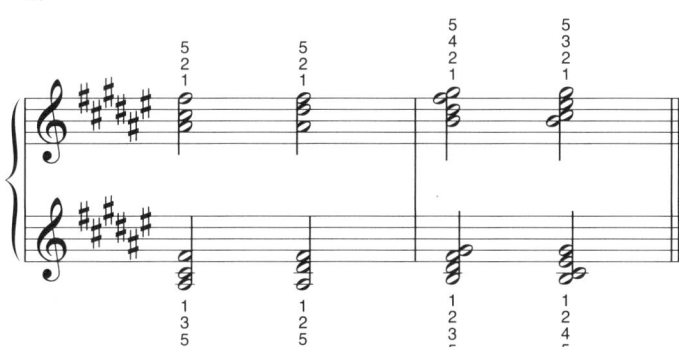

3.

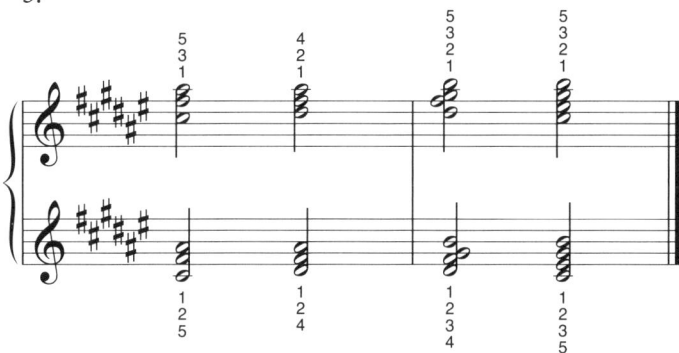

4.

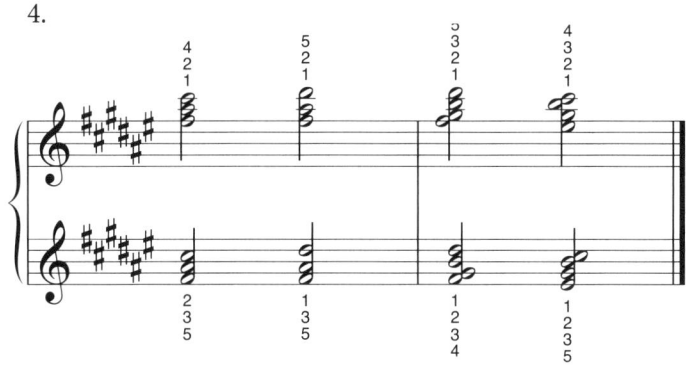

Technical Exercises

Group B: Chords | Key of G major | ♩ = 100

You must prepare the following major chord sequences with both right and left hands separately. The examiner will select two consecutive chord sequences for you to play: e.g. 1 & 2, 2 & 3 or 3 & 4.

1.

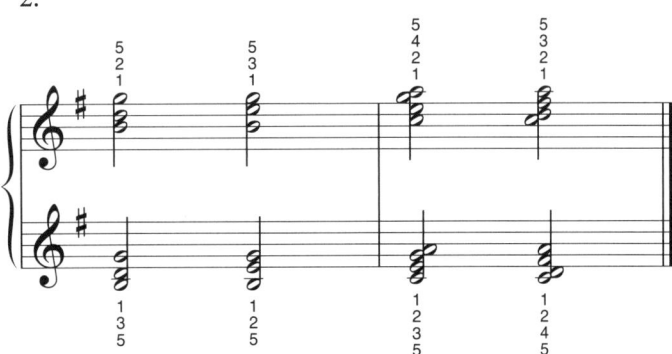

2.

3.

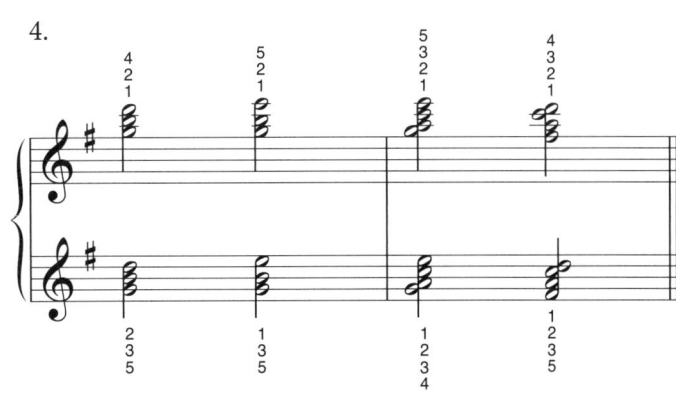

4.

Technical Exercises

Group B: Chords | Key of A♭ major | ♩=100

You must prepare the following major chord sequences with both right and left hands separately. The examiner will select two consecutive chord sequences for you to play: e.g. 1 & 2, 2 & 3 or 3 & 4.

1.
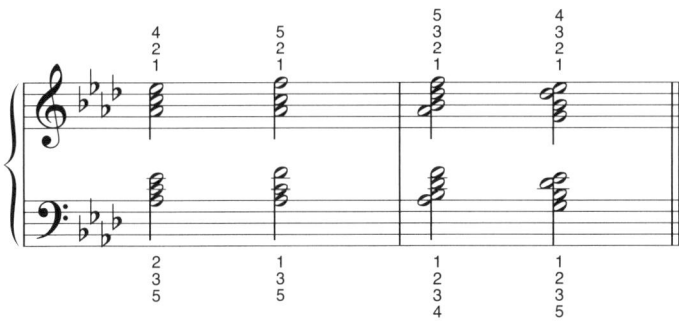

2.

3.
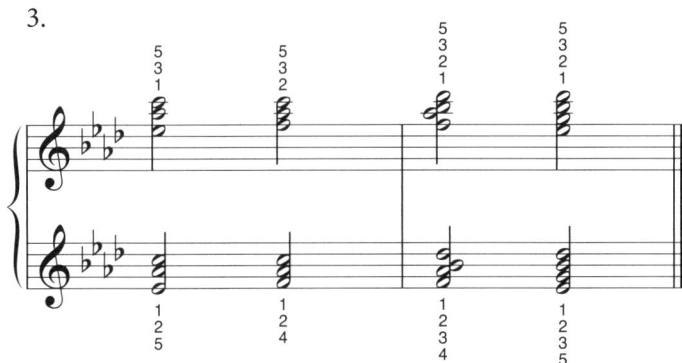

4.
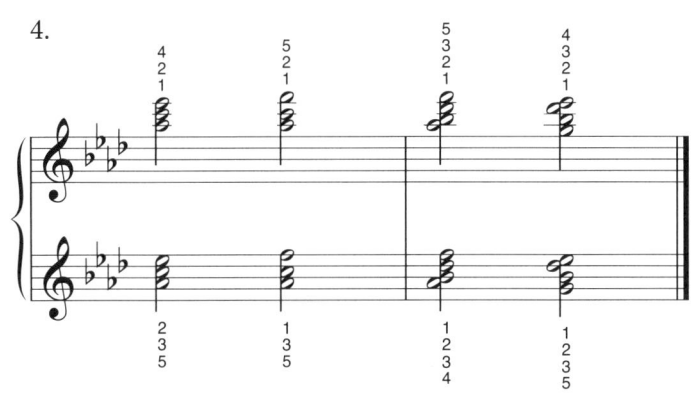

Technical Exercises

Group B: Chords | Key of A major | ♩=100

You must prepare the following major chord sequences with both right and left hands separately. The examiner will select two consecutive chord sequences for you to play: e.g. 1 & 2, 2 & 3 or 3 & 4.

1.
2.
3.
4.

Technical Exercises

Group B: Chords | Key of B♭ major | ♩=100

You must prepare the following major chord sequences with both right and left hands separately. The examiner will select two consecutive chord sequences for you to play: e.g. 1 & 2, 2 & 3 or 3 & 4.

1.

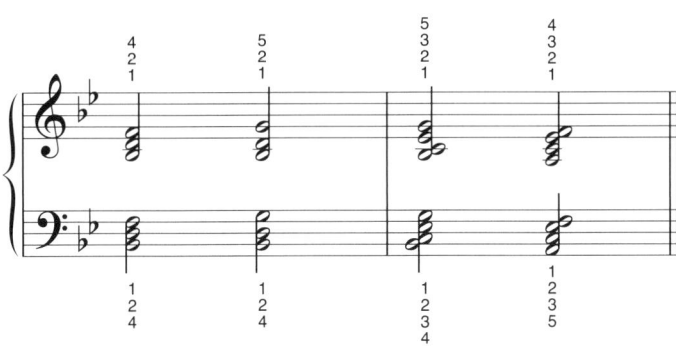

2.

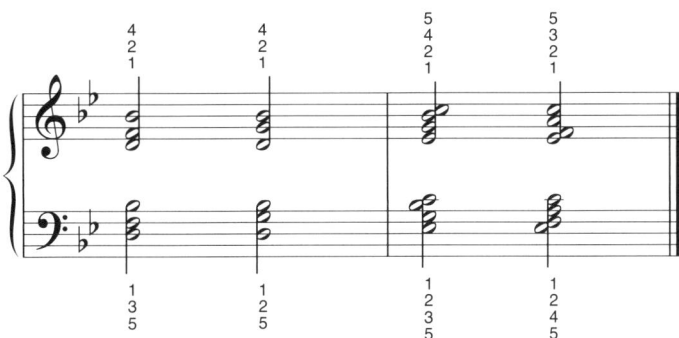

3.

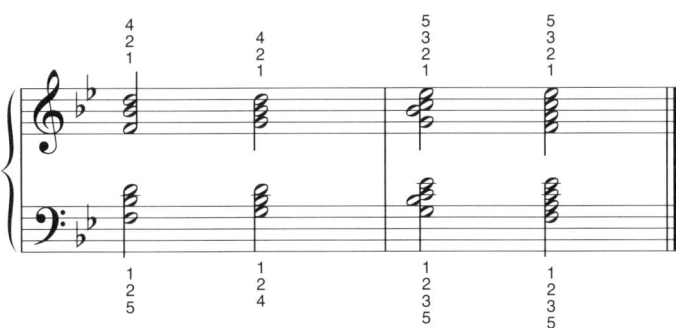

4.

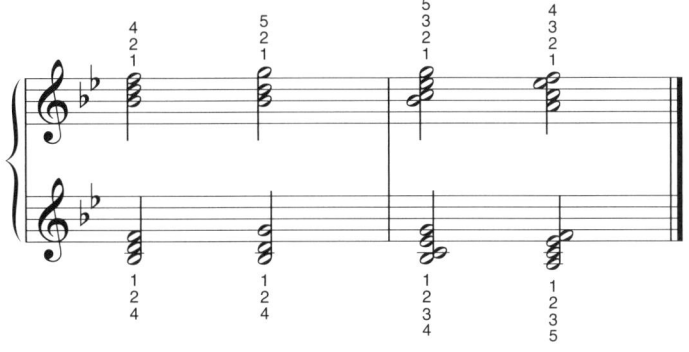

Technical Exercises

Group B: Chords | Key of B major | ♩=100

You must prepare the following major chord sequences with both right and left hands separately. The examiner will select two consecutive chord sequences for you to play: e.g. 1 & 2, 2 & 3 or 3 & 4.

1.

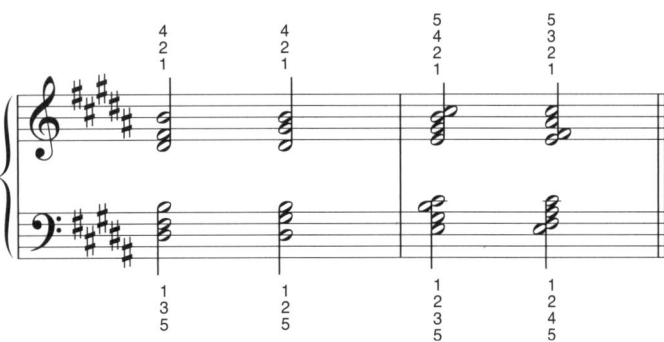

2.

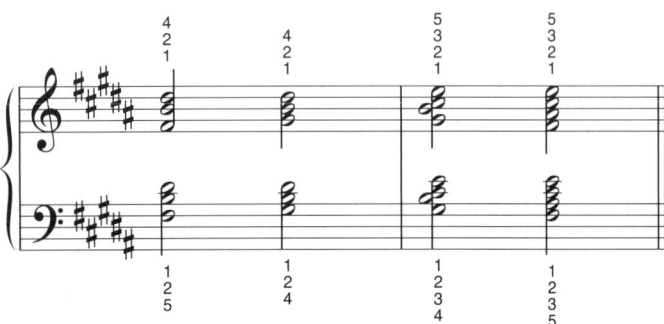

3.

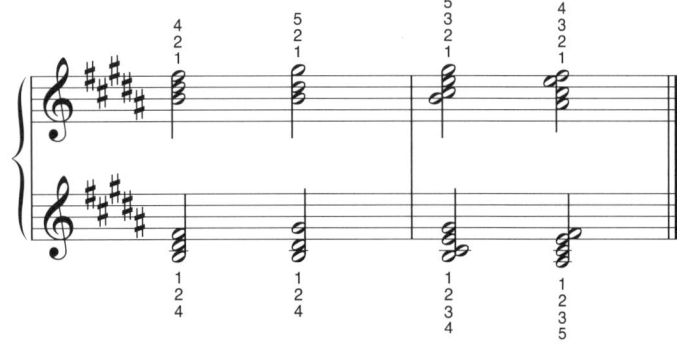

4.

Technical Exercises

Group C | Major sevenths | ♩=135

1a. F# major⁷ exercise

1b. G major⁷ exercise

1c. A♭ major⁷ exercise

Technical Exercises

1d. A major⁷ exercise

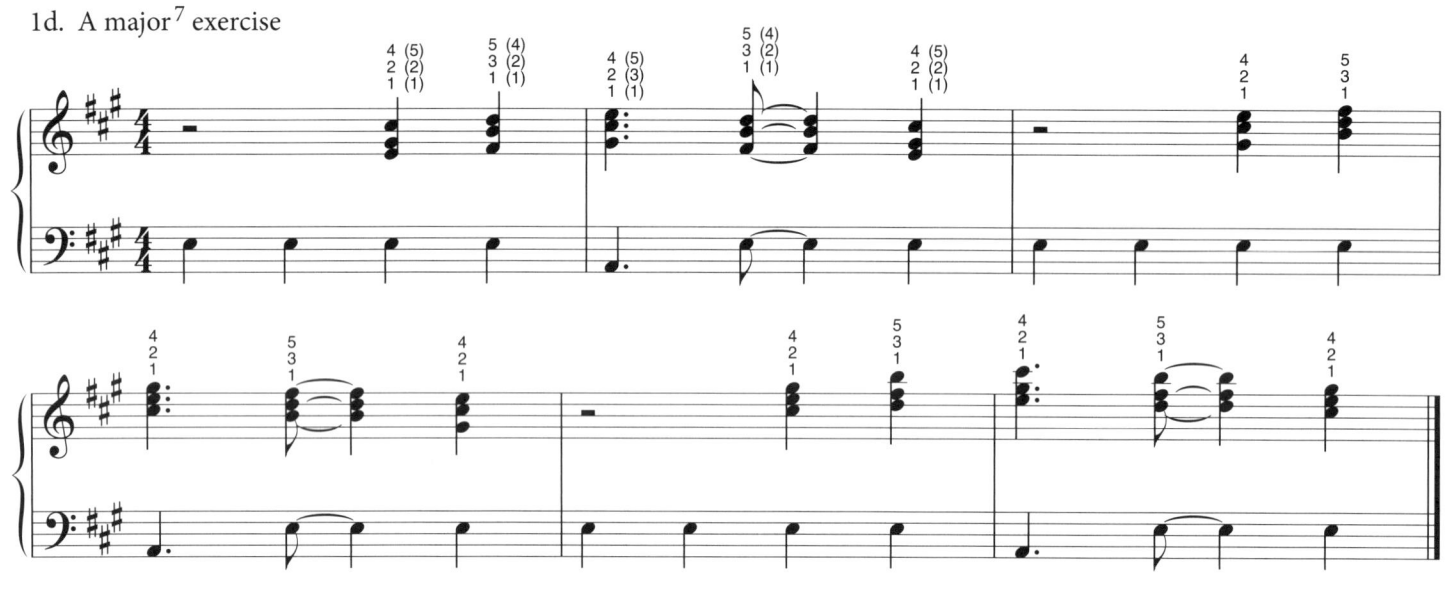

1e. B♭ major⁷ exercise

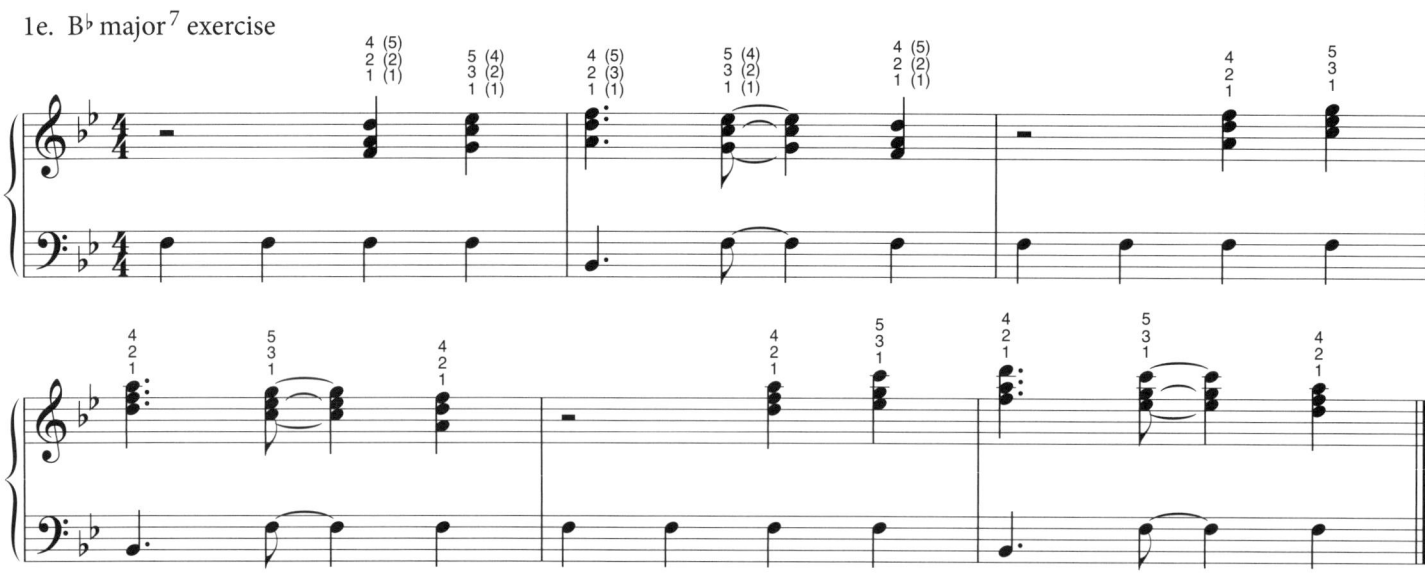

1f. B major⁷ exercise

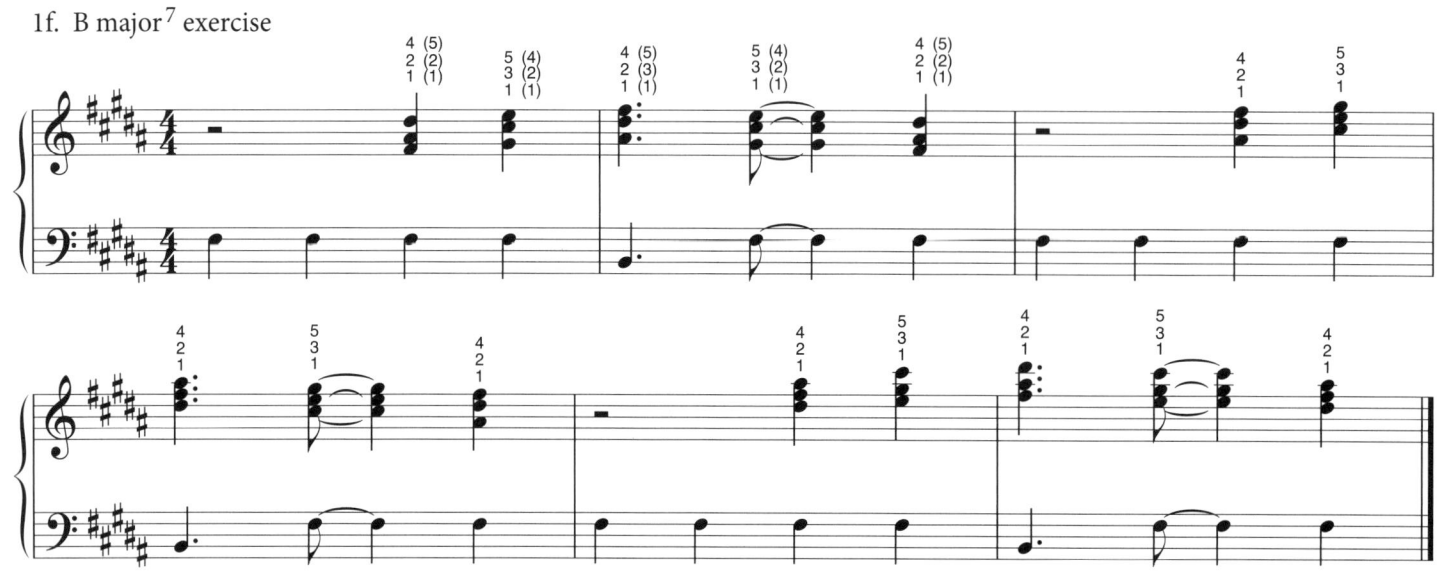

Technical Exercises

Group D: Riff | ♩=135

In the exam you will be asked to play the following riff to the backing track found on the BBK candidate book CD. The riff shown in bar 1 should be played in the same shape in the bars 2–8. The root note of the pattern to be played is shown in the music in each bar where the chord changes. Where only one bar is shown play only the first bar of the riff.

Sight Reading

Candidates attempting Grades 1–5 inclusive have a choice of taking either the sight reading or the improvisation & interpretation test in the exam. There is no improvisation and interpretation option at Debut grade as all candidates must take the sight reading test. Six examples of the types of tests required in the exam are shown below. The full technical specifications of each test offered to candidates in the exam can be found in the BBK *Syllabus Guide*. Please note that in Grades 4 and 5 each sight reading test also contains two bars of improvisation & interpretation.

You will be asked to prepare a sight reading test which is given to you by the examiner. The examiner will allow you 90 seconds to prepare for the test and will set the tempo on a metronome. You can choose to play with or without the metronome.

Practice and preparation

Unfortunately, most candidates don't look forward to this part of the exam. However, there is so much to be gained from being able to look at a piece of music you have not seen before and play it.

In the exam the most important aspect of the test is to see if you can recognise the 'shape' of the music and maintain fluency. Success in these areas will earn a pass. The more of the test that is correct over and above these points the higher the mark.

Sight reading success comes from practice, but it's also important to refine a process that you follow *every* time you sight-read a piece of music. Work through the stages below when you look at piece of music for the first time:

Step 1 | Identifying time signature and patch

Before looking at the notes, look at the information on and above the stave just before the first bar of the music. Here you will find the time signature and the required keyboard sound patch.

Step 2 | Identifying identical, or similar bars

Most music is made up of repetition. Take the time to look for the bars that are the same or similar. This way you are immediately cutting down the number of bars you need to work on.

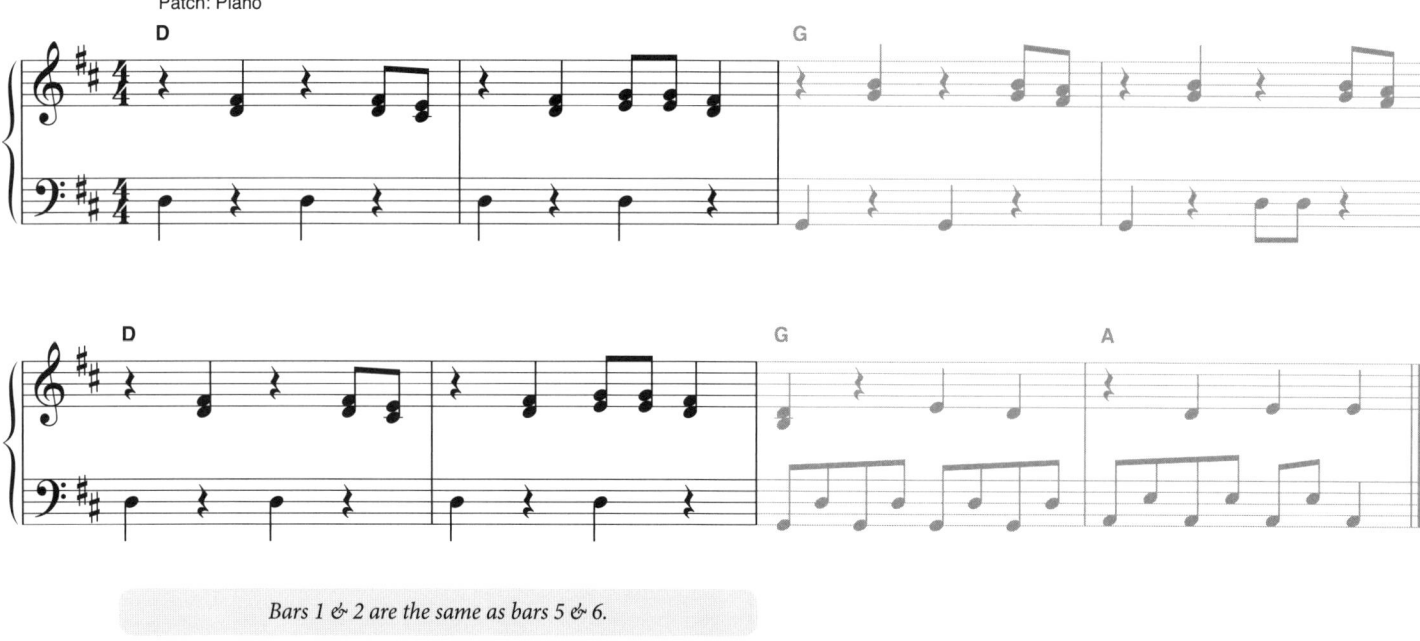

Bars 1 & 2 are the same as bars 5 & 6.

Step 3 | Identifying identical or similar rhythms

Most popular music is made up of repeated or similar rhythms. Once you have identified them, work out how they sound.

- Bars 5 & 6 are identical to bars 1 & 2
- Bars 3 & 4 have a similar rhythm

Step 4 | Practising rhythms

Tap, clap or play the rhythms on one note. This helps you learn how the notes will sound.

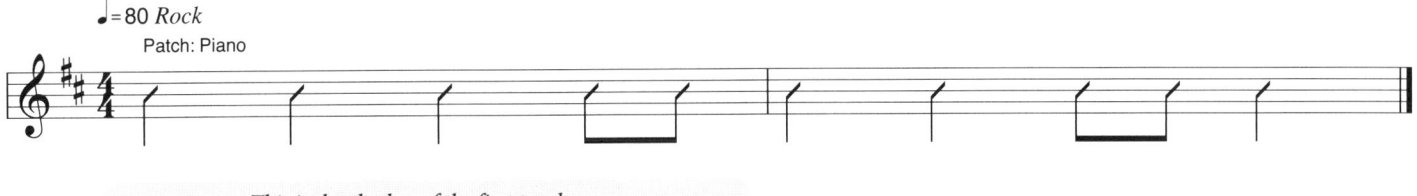

This is the rhythm of the first two bars.

Sight Reading

Step 5 | Identify key signature and pitch range

Look at the key signature and then find the lowest and highest notes in the piece. This will help you select the correct hand position and anticipate any stretches you might encounter.

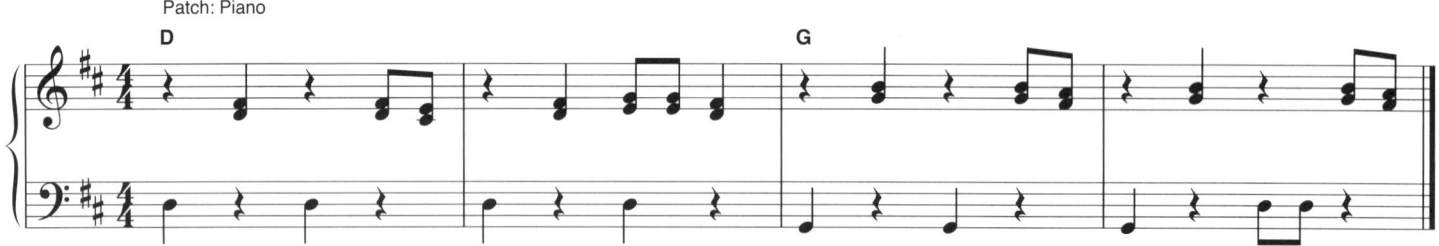

- *The key signature is D major. All F and C notes are sharpened (played a semi-tone higher).*
- *The lowest note in the right hand is C♯ and the highest B so there is the need to stretch one note either side of the natural five-finger range.*
- *In the left hand the lowest note is G and the highest is D. This fits into the five-finger range.*

Step 6 | Practise similar bars

With only a limited amount of time to prepare the test it is advisable to start by practising those few bars that likely make up the bulk of the piece.

Stage 7 | Practise different bars

Finally, practise any bars that are different. These stages can be achieved quickly with practise. It is simply a matter of training the eye to speed read these points.

The Exam

You will be given 90 seconds to prepare the piece. Make sure you read the syllabus guide or the back of your grade book as the keys are set for each grade, so you should be totally familiar with the keys you will be presented.

The examiner will offer you the metronome for the practise time or as a four-beat indication of the tempo. Choose the one that works best for you. It's best to stick with the method you have used in your exam preparation at home. The examiner will offer you the metronome for the performance.

Remember the process outlined above. Here is a brief summary:
- identify the time signature and patch
- look for the bars that are the same or similar
- look for the rhythms that are the same or similar and tap/clap/play them
- look at the key signature and the lowest and highest notes
- practise the similar bars
- practise the other bars

You will achieve the higher marks for maintaining fluency throughout the test. This, after all, is what would be expected in 'real' live performance.

Sight Reading

Debut

The following examples are indicative of the types of test you will be given in the Debut exam.

All exercises are to be played at the tempo ♩ = 60

Example 1

Example 2

Example 3

Sight Reading

Example 4

Example 5

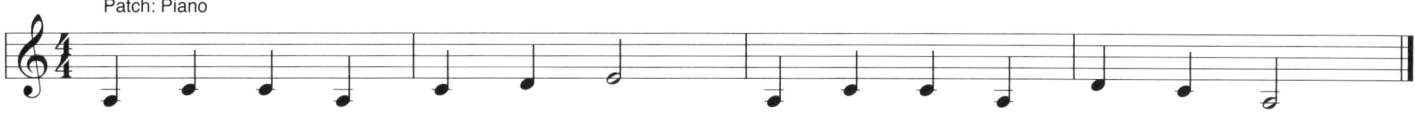

Example 6

Sight Reading

Grade 1

The following examples are indicative of the types of test you will be given in the Grade 1 exam.

All exercises are to be played at the tempo ♩ = **70**

Example 1

Example 2

Example 3

Sight Reading

Example 4

Example 5

Example 6

Sight Reading

Grade 2

The following examples are indicative of the types of test you will be given in the Grade 2 exam.

All exercises are to be played at the tempo ♩=70

Example 1

Pop
Patch: Electric Piano

Example 2

Rock
Patch: Piano

Example 3

Funk
Patch: Electric Piano

Sight Reading

Example 4

Rock
Patch: Piano

Example 5

Pop
Patch: Electric Piano

Example 6

Funk
Patch: Electric Piano

Sight Reading

Grade 3

The following examples are indicative of the types of test you will be given in the Grade 3 exam.

Example 1

Example 2

Example 3

Sight Reading

Example 4

Example 5

Example 6

Sight Reading

Grade 4

The following examples are indicative of the types of test you will be given in the Grade 4 exam. Please note that in Grade 4, the sight reading tests contain a small amount of improvisation & interpretation. This consists of a two-bar section at the end of each test.

Example 1

Example 2

Sight Reading

Example 3

Example 4

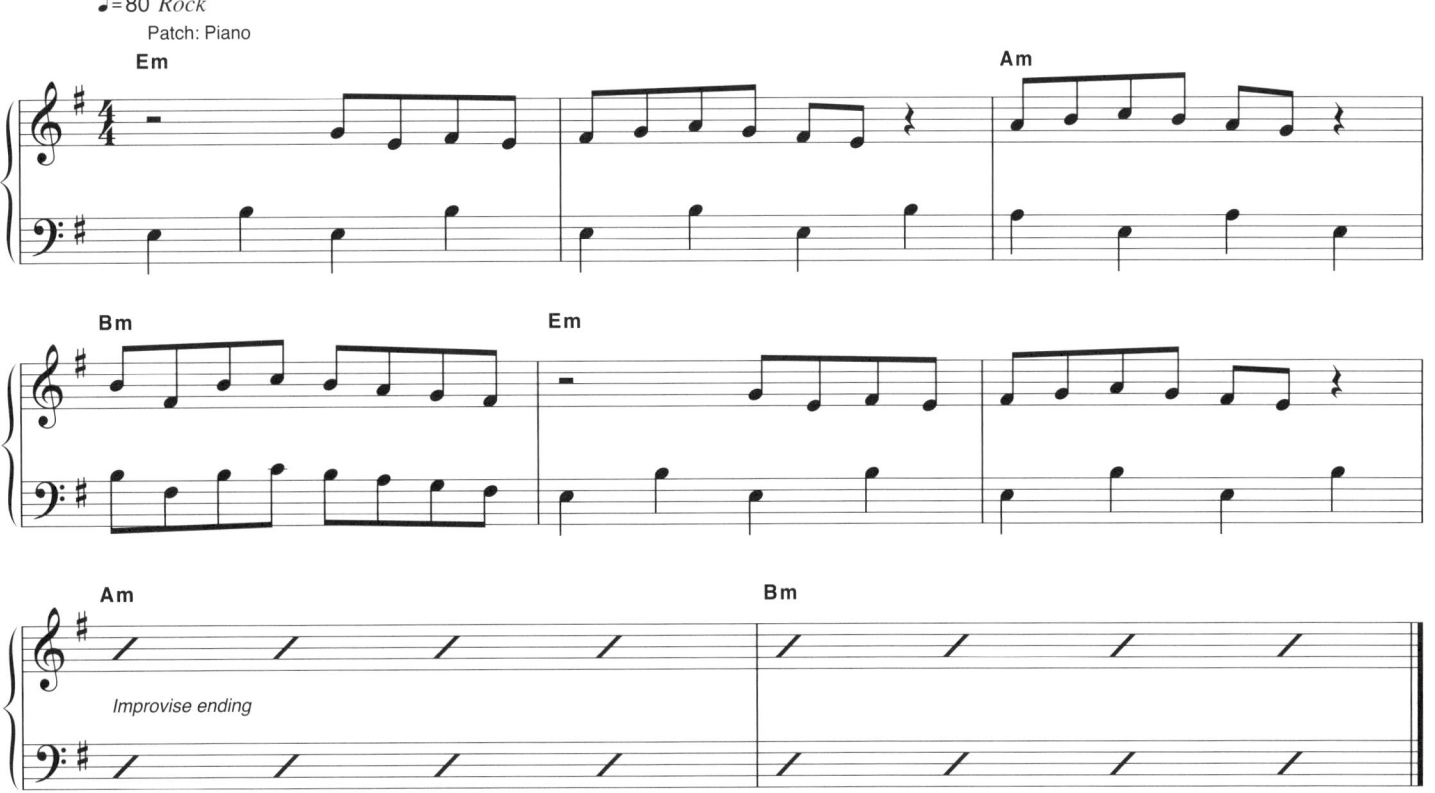

Sight Reading

Example 5

Example 6

Sight Reading

Grade 5

The following examples are indicative of the types of test you will be given in the Grade 5 exam. Please note that in Grade 5, the sight reading tests contain a small amount of improvisation & interpretation. This consists of a two-bar section at the end of each test.

Example 1

Example 2

Sight Reading

Example 3

Example 4

Sight Reading

Example 5

♩=100 *Funk*
Patch: Electric Piano

Example 6

♩=90 *Jazz*
Patch: Piano

Improvisation & Interpretation

Candidates attempting Grades 1–5 inclusive have a choice of taking either the sight reading or the improvisation & interpretation test in the exam. There is no improvisation and interpretation option at Debut grade as all candidates must take the sight reading test. Six examples of the types of tests required in the exam are shown below. The full technical specifications of each test offered to candidates in the exam can be found in the BBK *Syllabus Guide*. Please note that in Grades 4 and 5 each improvisation & interpretation test also contains two bars of sight reading.

Practice and Preparation

The ability to improvise is a great asset in popular music. With so many sections of popular music repeated it's good to be able to vary aspects your performances.

The important thing to remember is that improvisation does not mean that every bar has to be different or that every beat has to be filled. Learning to develop material and to leave gaps will sound much better than frantically playing lots of different ideas.

Use these simple steps:

Step 1 | Look at the chord symbols

Take the time to look at the chord symbols. Most popular music is made of repeated chord progressions. If you identify these you will see there are fewer different bars to deal with than you may think.

1. Identify the repeated chords – in this case the G chords are repeated

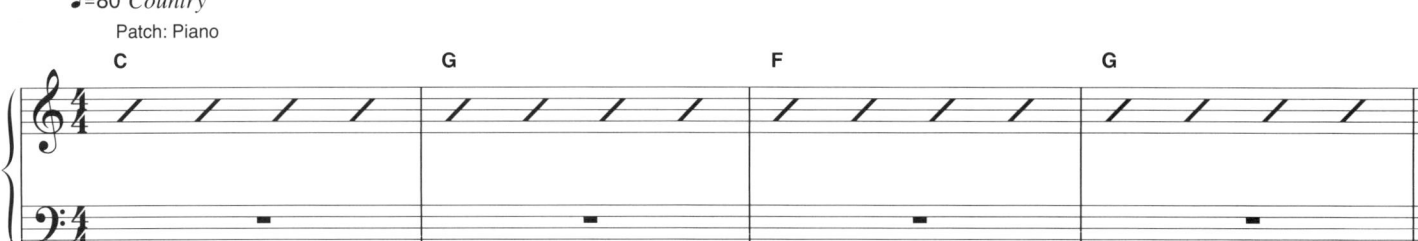

Step 2 | Simplify the chords

Play through the chords and identify the chord inversions that are closest to the one another. This is called 'voice leading'. Moving between root position chords will give your improvisations a disjointed feel.

2. Chord sequence played in root position chords

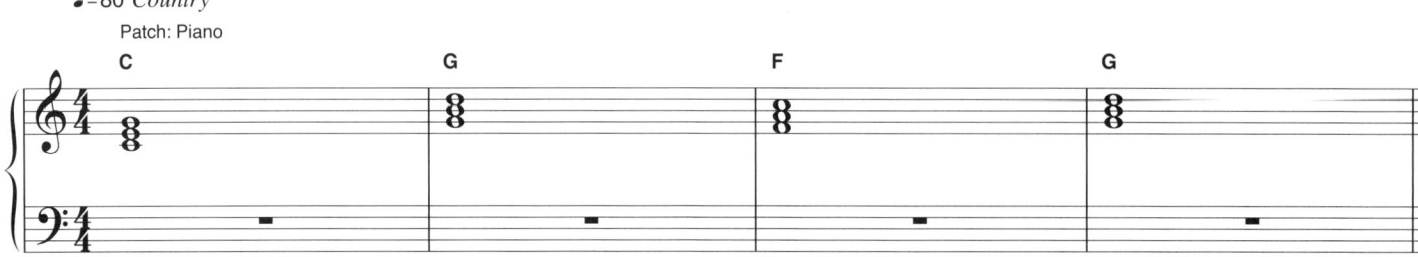

3. Chord Sequence played using inversions – voice leading

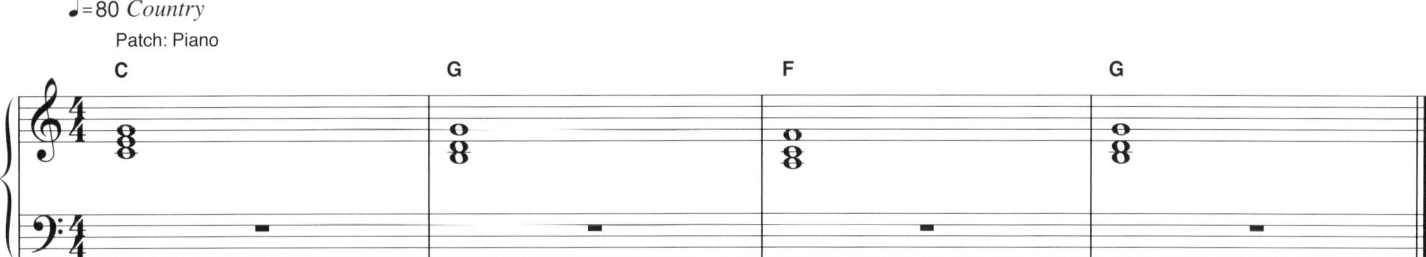

Read the syllabus guide or the examples in the back of your grade book: these tell you the specific keys and chords used at each grade. You should be thoroughly familiar with them before the exam.

Step 3 | Rhythmic patterns

Learn some basic rhythmic patterns that work. For example, playing the right hand on all four beats will sound laboured and dull (Ex. 4). One of the most popular rhythms will be on beats 2 and 4. This gives a sense of beat and direction (Ex. 5).

4. Right hand chords played on every beat

5. Right hand chords played on beats 2 and 4

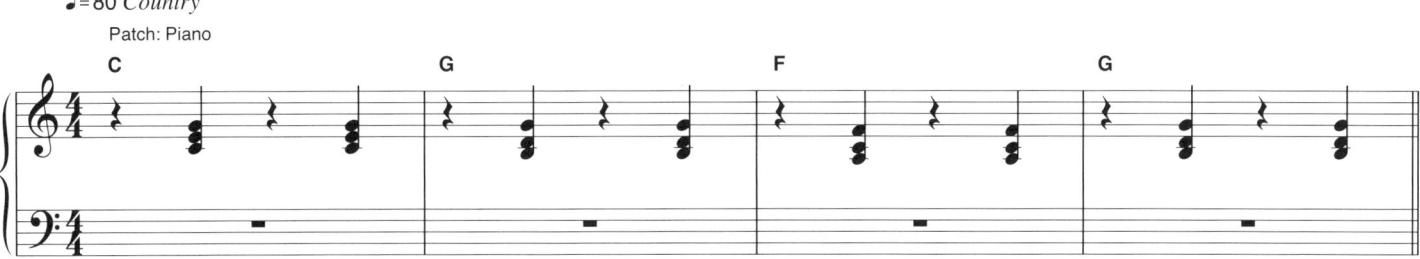

6. Right Hand chords played on beats 2 and 4 with left hand added

Improvisation & Interpretation

Step 4 | Creating a strong left hand part

If you use the left hand it's best to play mainly the root and fifth of the chord. The third has a tendency to sound weak.

7. Using the root and fifth of a chord for the left hand part

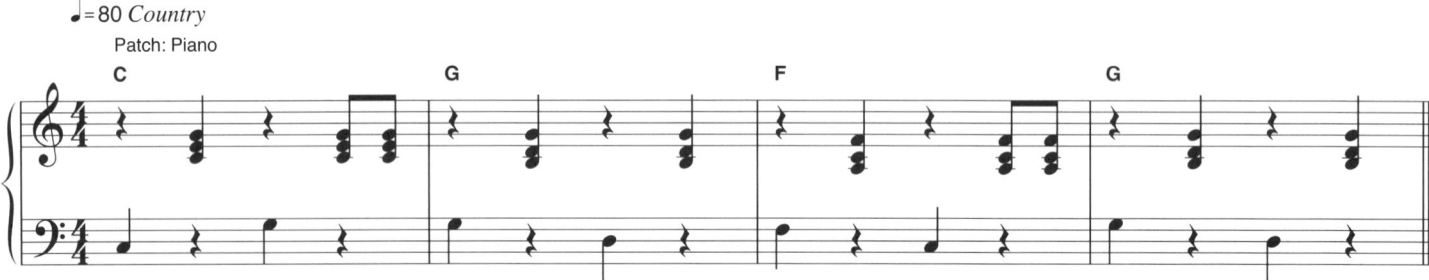

Step 5 | Develop something simple and memorable

Begin by adding small changes in rhythm and make sure that you choose something that you can remember. Eight bars of different rhythms and/or melodic ideas will sound disjointed and rambling: keep it simple!

8. Developing the left hand rhythm

The Exam

The examiner will show you the piece and then give you 30 seconds to prepare some ideas. This is enough time to note the similar bars of chords and to secure the chord positions. You will be given the opportunity to practise with or without the metronome. If you choose to practise without it, four beats will be given to show you the tempo. Practising with the metronome is encouraged as the mind often imagines a faster tempo and this can lead to rehearsals of ideas that don't always work at the correct, slower tempo. Keep your ideas simple so that you can hear and feel the beat as you play. It is often a good idea to just listen to the pulse on the metronome for a few bars to establish the tempo.

You will get the opportunity to practise through with the backing track once for rehearsal and then repeat it for the exam. In the rehearsal make sure your ideas are simple as this will give you the chance to settle into the piece and gain confidence. On the repeat you might find it easier to add more complex ideas. The most important thing is that you keep going. Don't stop, even if you feel things are going badly.

Improvisation & Interpretation

Grade 1

You will be asked to play an improvised line to a backing track of four bars. You have 30 seconds to prepare and then you will be allowed to practise through on the first playing of the backing track, before playing it to the examiner on the second playing of the backing track. This test is continuous with a one bar count in at the beginning and after the practice session.

All exercises are to be played at the tempo ♩=70

Example 1   CD 1 Track 1

Funk
Patch: Piano

Example 2   CD 1 Track 2

Rock
Patch: Organ

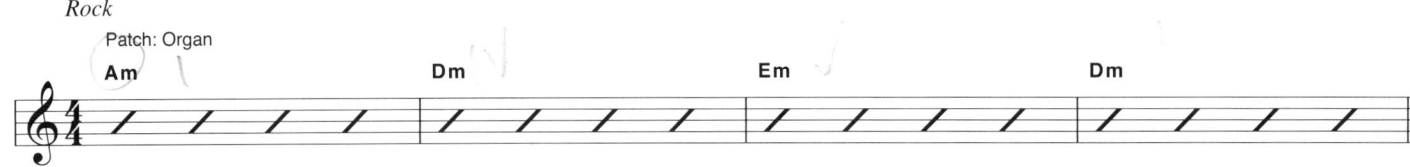

Example 3   CD 1 Track 3

Country
Patch: Piano

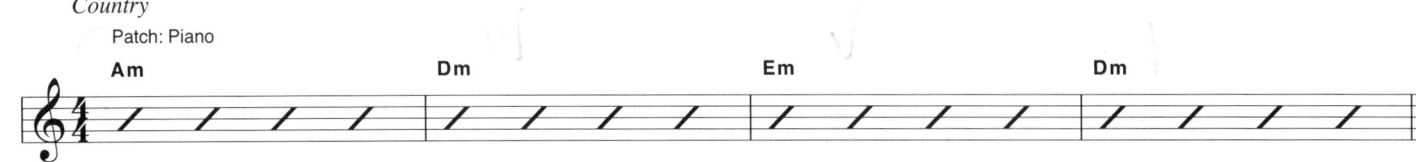

Improvisation & Interpretation

Example 4   CD 1 Track 4

Example 5   CD 1 Track 5

Example 6   CD 1 Track 6

Improvisation & Interpretation

Grade 2

You will be asked to play an improvised line to a backing track of four bars. You have 30 seconds to prepare and then you will be allowed to practise through on the first playing of the backing track, before playing it to the examiner on the second playing of the backing track. This test is continuous with a one bar count in at the beginning and after the practice session.

All exercises are to be played at the tempo ♩=80

Example 1   CD 1 Track 7

Country
Patch: Piano

Example 2   CD 1 Track 8

Funk
Patch: Organ

Example 3   CD 1 Track 9

Pop
Patch: Piano

Improvisation & Interpretation

Example 4   CD 1 Track 10

Rock
Patch: Organ

Example 5   CD 1 Track 11

Pop
Patch: Piano

Example 6   CD 1 Track 12

Funk
Patch: Organ

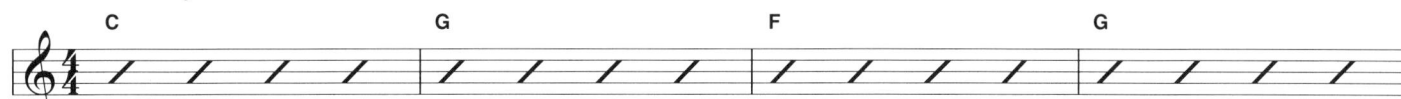

Improvisation & Interpretation

Grade 3

You will be asked to play an improvised line to a backing track of eight bars. You have 30 seconds to prepare and then you will be allowed to practise through on the first playing of the backing track, before playing it to the examiner on the second playing of the backing track. This test is continuous with a one bar count in at the beginning and after the practice session.

Example 1   CD 1 Track 13

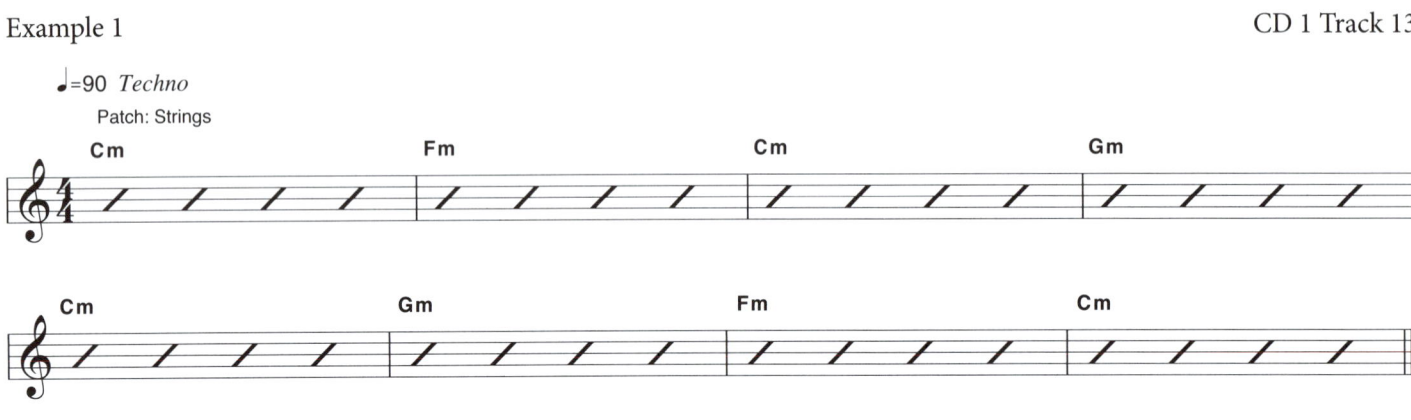

Example 2   CD 1 Track 14

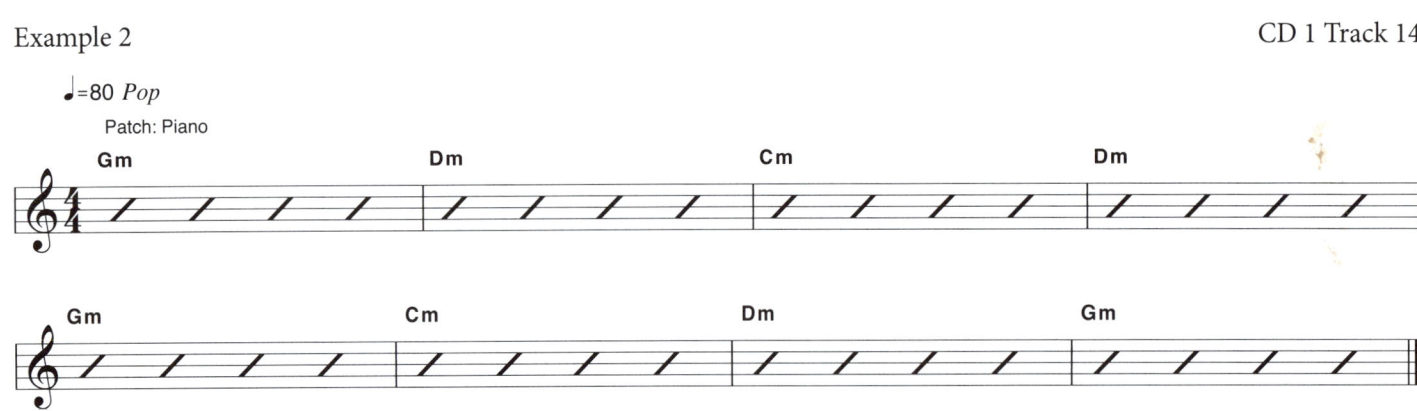

Example 3   CD 1 Track 15

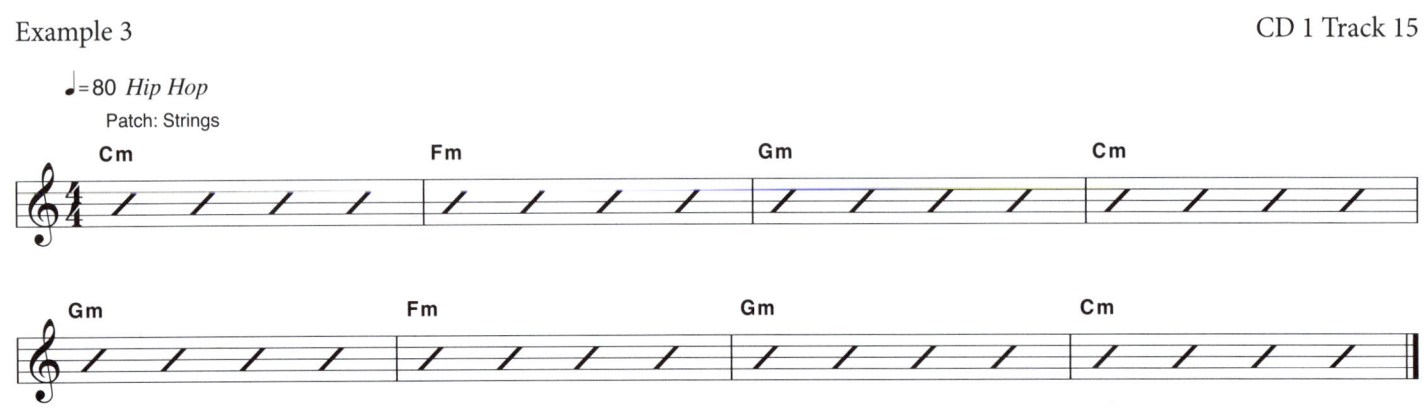

Improvisation & Interpretation

Example 4   CD 1 Track 16

♩=85 *Pop*
Patch: Strings

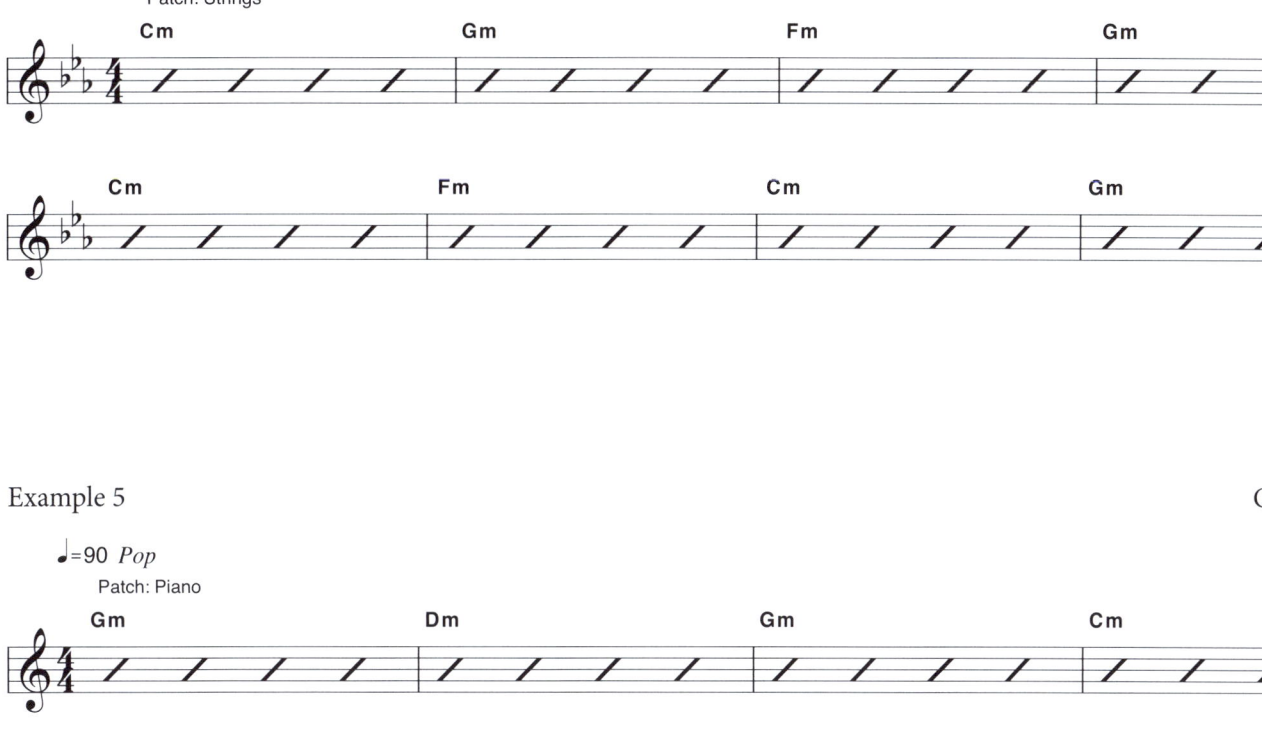

Example 5   CD 1 Track 17

♩=90 *Pop*
Patch: Piano

Example 6   CD 1 Track 18

♩=80 *Smooth Jazz*
Patch: Piano

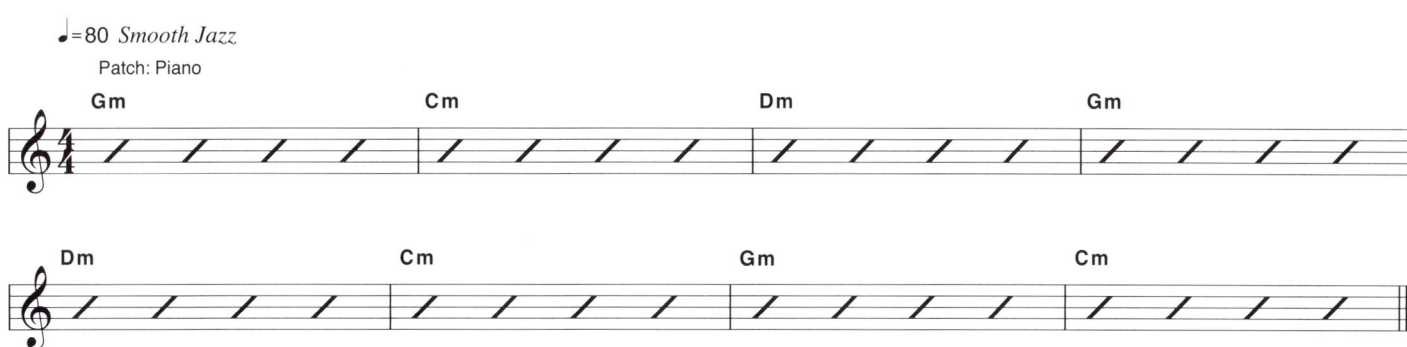

Improvisation & Interpretation

Grade 4

At Grade 4 there is an element of sight reading. This takes the form of a two-bar rhythm at the beginning of the test. You will be asked to play the chords in the given rhythm and continue an improvised line using chords where indicated by the chord chart and using either the organ or electric piano patch on your keyboard. Note that an element of left-hand work is expected at this grade. You will be allowed 30 seconds to prepare. You will be allowed to practise through one playing of the test on the CD before playing it a second time for the exam. This test is continuous with a one-bar count in at the beginning and after the practice session. The key will be either C major or F major and will use chords I, ii7, IV, V and vi.

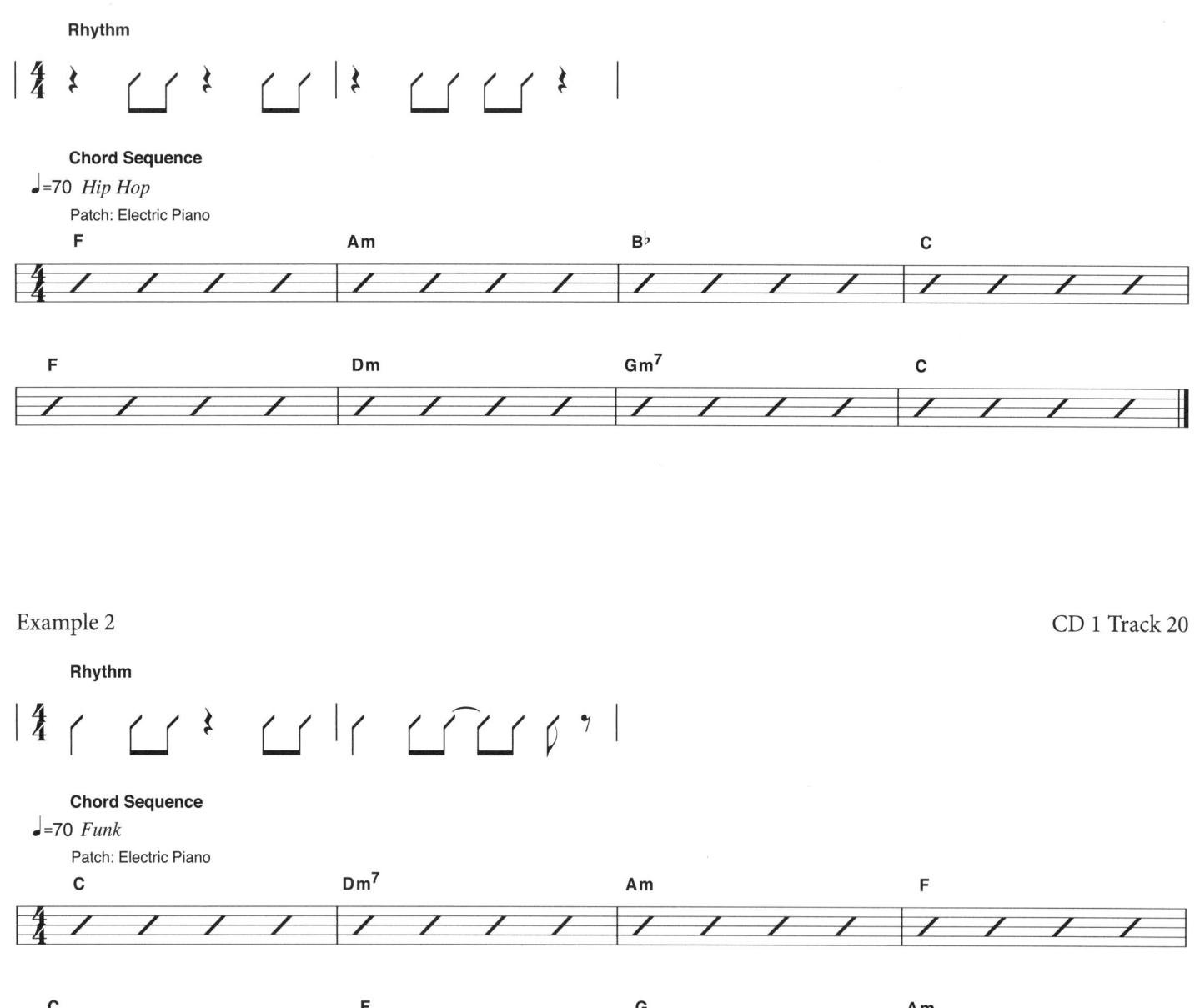

Improvisation & Interpretation

Example 3
CD 1 Track 21

Rhythm

Chord Sequence
♩=70 *Rock*
Patch: Organ

| C | F | Am | G |
| Am | G | Dm7 | G |

Example 4
CD 1 Track 22

Rhythm

Chord Sequence
♩=70 *Ballad*
Patch: Electric Piano

| F | Gm7 | F | B♭ |
| F | Dm | B♭ | C |

Improvisation & Interpretation

Example 5 CD 1 Track 23

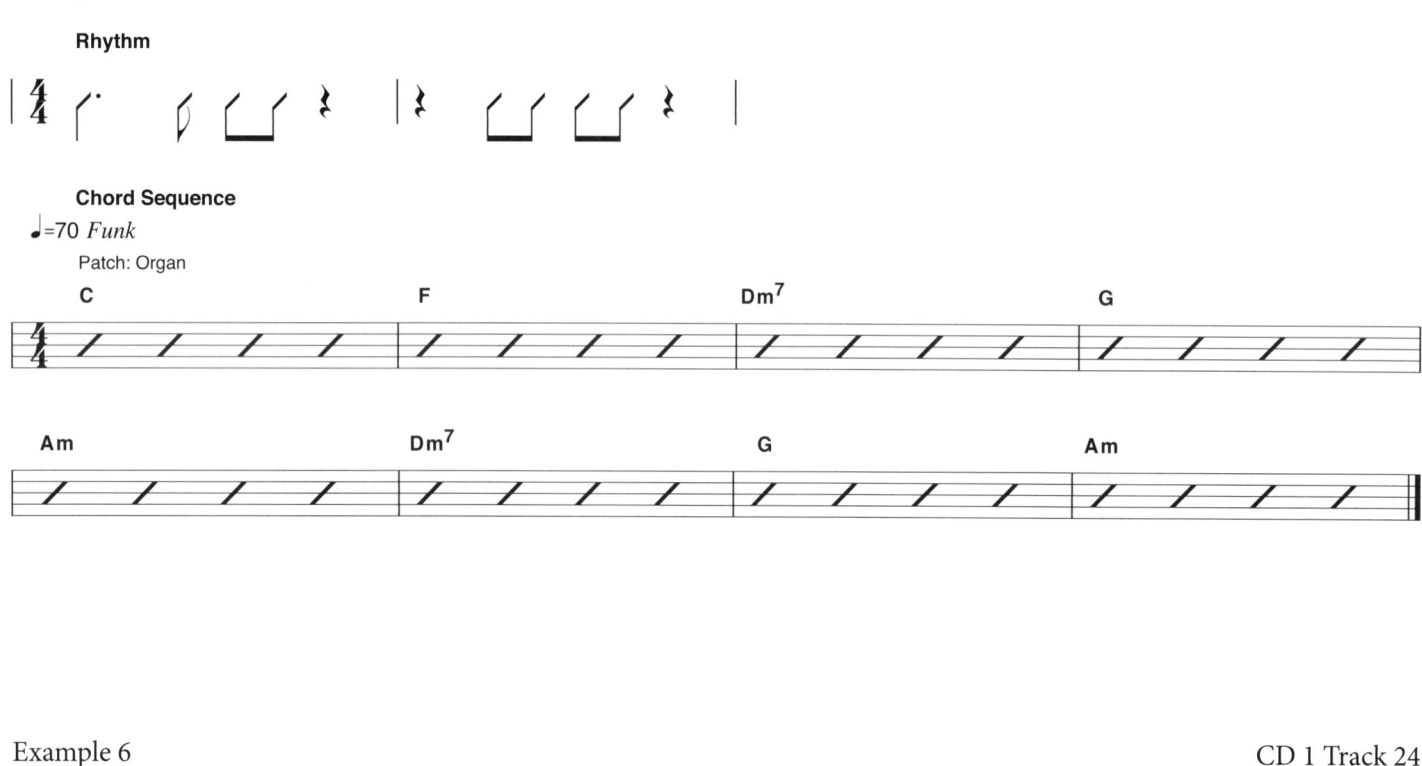

Example 6 CD 1 Track 24

Improvisation & Interpretation

Grade 5

At Grade 5 there is an element of sight reading. This takes the form of a two-bar, chord-based riff at the beginning of the test. You will be asked to play the chords in the given rhythm and continue an improvised line using chords and melody where indicated by the chord chart using either the electric piano or organ patch on your keyboard. You will be allowed 30 seconds to prepare. You will be allowed to practise through one playing of the test on the CD before playing it a second time for the exam. This test is continuous with a one-bar count in at the beginning and after the practice session. The improvisation & interpretation test will be in the keys of either G minor or A minor.

Example 1 — CD 1 Track 25

Example 2 — CD 1 Track 26

Improvisation & Interpretation

Example 3 CD 1 Track 27

Example 4 CD 1 Track 28

Improvisation & Interpretation

Example 5   CD 1 Track 29

Example 6   CD 1 Track 30

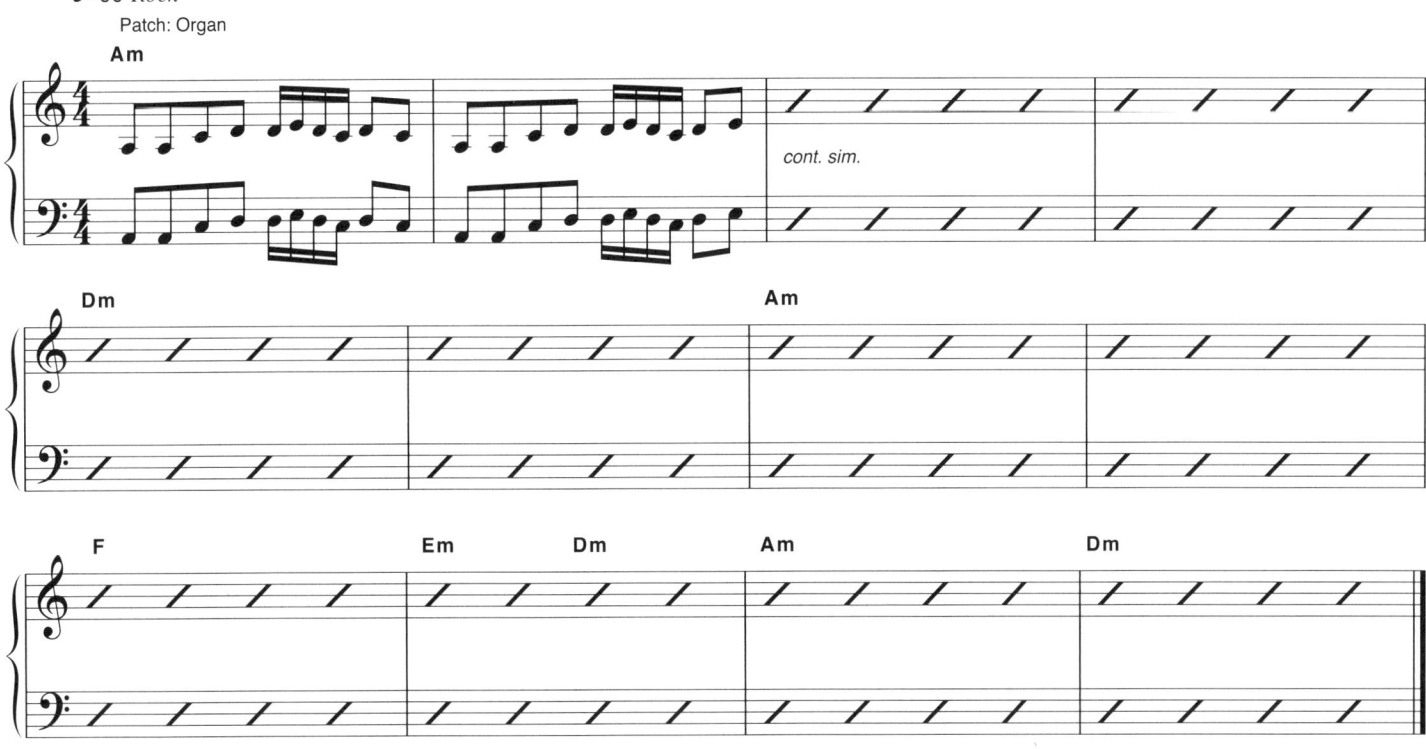

Ear Tests

Ear tests are nearer the end of the exam and can feel unnecessarily difficult due to the pressure of the exam. Ear tests are extremely important to a musician's training. They help develop the ability to identify melodic lines and harmonic (chords) relationships. If you are able to listen to a track and reproduce it, you instantly have access to a wealth of music. Not only this, but you are able to listen to a current favourite and, without waiting for the notation to be printed, you are able to play it.

Melodic recall

If you have been working through the other areas in this companion guide, you will already know there is a certain amount of repetition in music. This follows through to melodic work. In Debut the repetition is that the melody imitates the simple rhythm given in the first part of the test. This is because rhythm is the bedrock of music and should be one of the primary areas to focus on. The correct notes but in the wrong rhythm mean little, but a correct rhythm with some incorrect notes is often still identifiable. This is what candidate should aim for.

Melodies are often constructed of step-like movement (where the melody moves one scale note up or down at a time). This is what makes them memorable. They also have a shape: if the first half ascends, the second half will descend. If you consider these simple points, you will be very likely to achieve all or most of the test.

You will hear the test twice in the exam. One mistake many candidates make is to try to play along with the first playing. Whilst this is tempting, it is not going to be successful as you will not know what is coming. Take the first play through to establish these two areas:
- the rhythm
- the shape

You will be told the key and the starting note. Practice looking at the keyboard as the test is playing. Visualise the melody without creating any sounds. Let your eyes become your ears. This sounds complicated, but once you have practiced it, it is an invaluable tool.

1. Debut | Examples of Test 1 (above) & Test 2 (below)

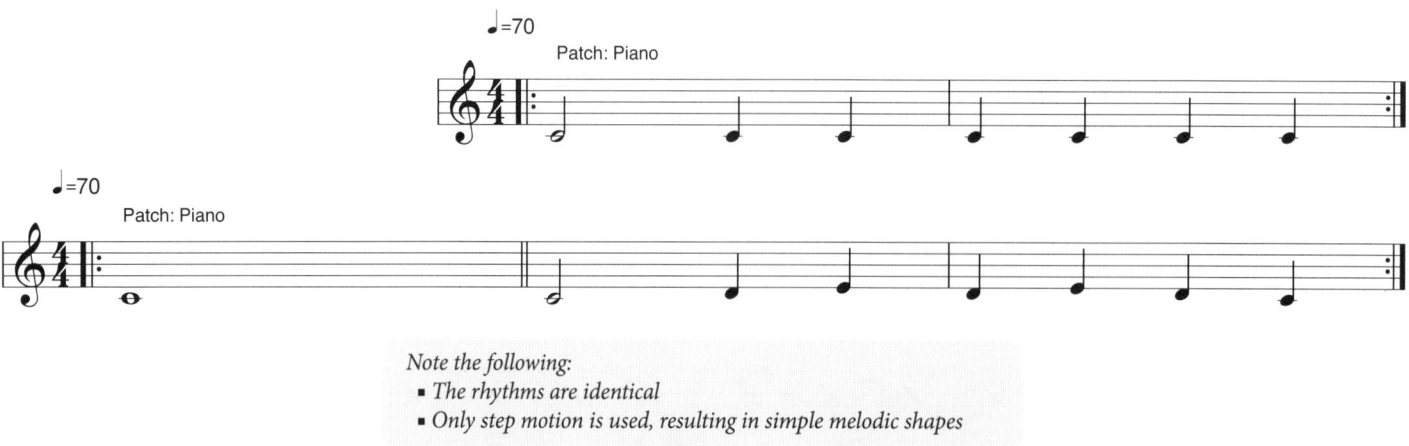

Note the following:
- *The rhythms are identical*
- *Only step motion is used, resulting in simple melodic shapes*

As the melodies get longer in the higher grades there will be repetition of bars. In the first play through try to identify where these happen. Generally they will be in bars 1 and 3.

2. Grade 3 | Example of Test 2

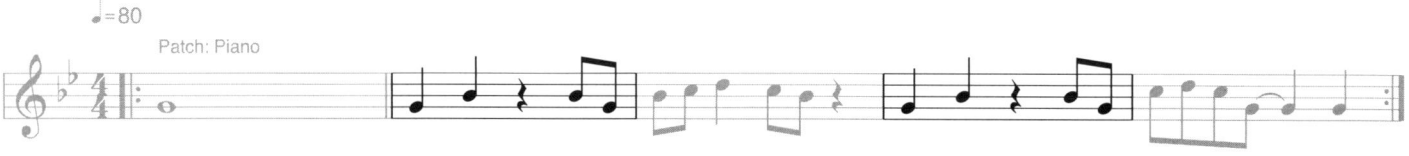

Note both the rhythmic and melodic repetition in bars 1 & 3 (highlighted).

It is also important to be able to identify melodies in the lower register. In grades 2 and 5, the tests are basslines. The same process applies, but you might consider playing them with your stronger hand.

3. Grade 2 | Example of Test 1

Rhythmic recall

This part of the test is designed to develop your ability to recognise rhythm and harmonic relationships with chords. In each grade the number of chords available is limited and so it is important you spend time familiarising yourself with the possibilities. They will be taken from the chords used in the technical exercises, either at the grade being taken or in any of the lower grades. Remember to practice changing chords using the nearest possible position (inversion) to ensure fluency. You will be told the first chord and the inversion, so you should be able to visualise the possible chord movements and inversions that may be used.

4. Chords used in Grade 1 | Test 2

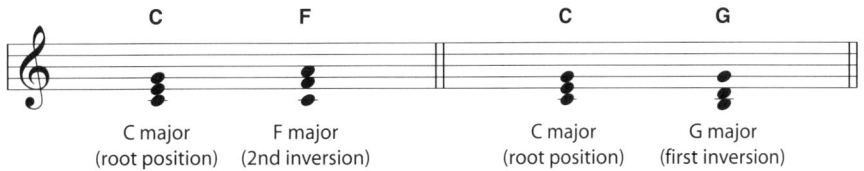

Learn the relationship between the tonic chord (in root position) and the other chords (and their inversions) that are used in the ear tests in the grade that you are studying.

In the exam you will hear each test twice and you should attempt to follow the same procedure as for the melodic recall. Part of this test is rhythmic recall, so avoid playing along with the first playing so that you can focus on all aspects of the test.

5. Grade 1 | Rhythmic Recall

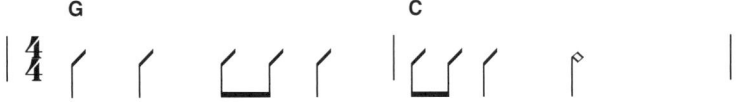

This example shows a Grade 1 rhythmic recall test reduced down to its rhythmic values and chords only.

Some candidates try to establish where the chord changes occur first, particularly in the lower grades where the changes are less frequent, but this does not suit everybody.

Ear Tests

As the tests get longer, there are again bars that repeat and it is important to establish where these are

6. Identifying Repeats

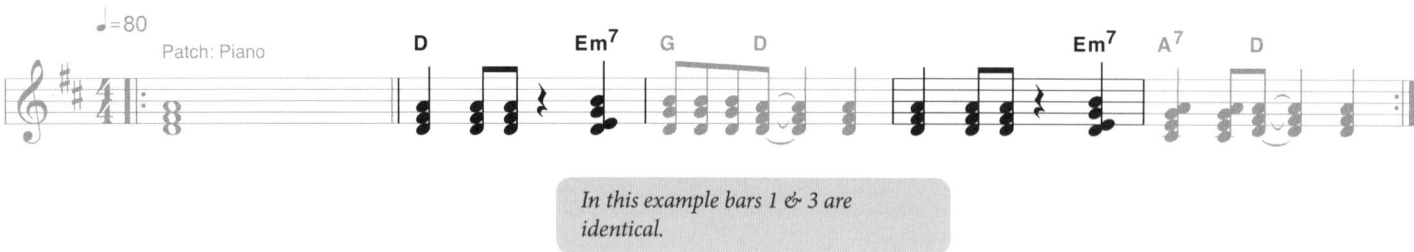

In this example bars 1 & 3 are identical.

In the longer tests it is vital that the rhythm is established before considering the chords.

The Exam

Debut

Test 1
- You will hear a two-bar rhythm played twice on middle C and then you will be required to play it back. You will hear it played twice with a drum backing and then there will be a break for you to practise. The test will begin again, and after a four-beat count in you will be required to play the rhythm with the drums.

Test 2
- You will hear a two-bar melody using the first three notes of C major sale in the same rhythm as test 1 and you will be required to play it back. You will hear it played twice with a drum backing and then there is a break for you to practice. The test will begin again and after a four beat count in you will be required to play the melody with the drums. The first note of the melody is always C.

Grades 1–5

Test 1
- You will hear a two/four-bar melody/bassline played twice. You will be required to play it back. You will hear it played twice with a drum backing and then there is a break for you to practice. The test will begin again and after a four-beat count in you will be required to play the melody with the drums. The examiner will tell you what the first note of the melody.

Test 2
- You will hear a two/four-bar chordal rhythm played twice and then you will be required to play it back. You will hear it played twice with a drum backing and then there will be a break for you to practice. The test will begin again, and after a four-beat count in you will be required to play the chords in the rhythm with the drums. The examiner will tell you the name of the first chord and its inversion.

Remember to identify:
- the rhythm
- the shape (visualising the notes on the keyboard)
- the nearest inversions

Ear Tests

Debut

Test 1 | Rhythmic Recall

You will be asked to play back using the piano patch on your keyboard a two-bar rhythm on the note middle C on your keyboard. You will hear the rhythm played twice with a drum backing. There will then be a short break for you to practise the test and then the test will recommence and you will be required to play the rhythm to the drum backing. This test is continuous.

Test 2 | Melodic Recall

You will be asked to play back using the piano patch on your keyboard a simple melody of two bars composed from the first three notes of the C major scale using the same rhythm as test 1. You will be given the tonic note and told the starting note and you will hear the test twice with a drum backing. There will then be a short break for you to practise the test and then the test will recommence and you will be required to play the melody with the drum backing. This test is continuous.

Ear Tests

Example 3 | Tests 1 & 2 CD 1 Track 33

Example 4 | Tests 1 & 2 CD 1 Track 34

Example 5 | Tests 1 & 2 CD 1 Track 35

Example 6 | Tests 1 & 2 CD 1 Track 36

Ear Tests

Grade 1 | Test 1 | Melodic Recall

You will be asked to play back using the piano patch on your keyboard a simple two-bar melody composed from either the A minor or E minor pentatonic scales. You will be given the tonic note and told the starting note and you will hear the test twice with a drum backing. There will then be a short break for you to practise the test and then the test will recommence and you will be required to play the melody with the drum backing. This test is continuous.

Example 1   CD 1 Track 37

Example 2   CD 1 Track 38

Example 3   CD 1 Track 39

Ear Tests

Example 4   CD 1 Track 40

Example 5   CD 1 Track 41

Example 6   CD 1 Track 42

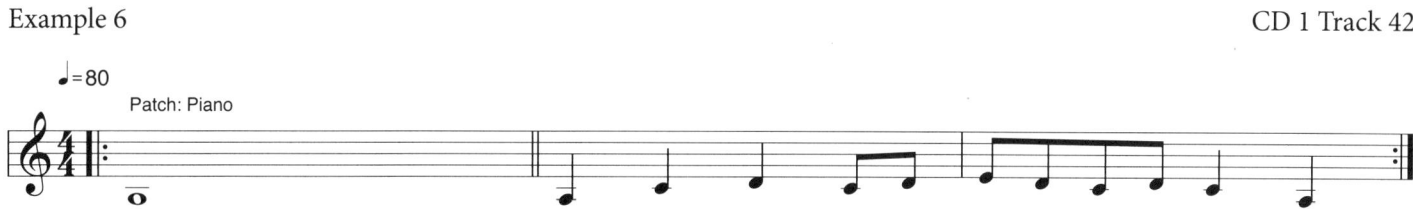

Ear Tests

Grade 1 | Test 2 | Chord and Rhythm Recall

You will be asked to play back using the piano patch on your keyboard a two-bar rhythmic chord sequence. You will be told the tonic chord, the first chord and inversion. You will hear the rhythmic chord sequence made up of chords I, IV and V in the key of C major or G major played twice with a drum backing. There will then be a short break for you to practise the test and then the test will recommence and you will be required to play the rhythmic chord sequence to the drum backing. This test is continuous.

Example 1   CD 1 Track 43

Example 2   CD 1 Track 44

Example 3   CD 1 Track 45

Ear Tests

Example 4   CD 1 Track 46

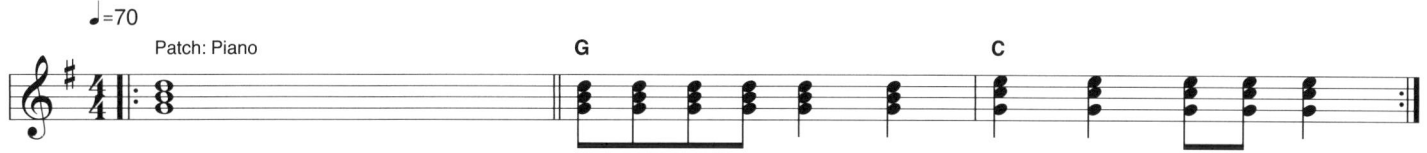

Example 5   CD 1 Track 47

Example 6   CD 1 Track 48

Ear Tests

Grade 2 | Test 1 | Melodic Recall

You will be asked to play back using the piano patch on your keyboard a simple two-bar bassline composed from either the G major or F major scales. You will be given the tonic note and told the starting note and you will hear the test twice with a drum backing. There will then be a short break for you to practise the test and then the test will recommence and you will be required to play the melody with the drum backing. This test is continuous.

Example 1   CD 1 Track 49

Example 2   CD 1 Track 50

Example 3   CD 1 Track 51

Ear Tests

Example 4   CD 1 Track 52

Example 5   CD 1 Track 53

Example 6   CD 1 Track 54

Ear Tests

Grade 2 | Test 2 | Chord and Rhythm Recall

You will be asked to play back using the piano patch on your keyboard a two-bar rhythmic chord sequence on your keyboard. You will be told the tonic chord, the first chord and the inversion, and you will hear the rhythmic chord sequence made up of chords i, iv and v in the key of A minor or D minor played twice with a drum backing. There will then be a short break for you to practise the test and then the test will recommence and you will be required to play the rhythmic chord sequence to the drum backing. This test is continuous.

Example 1   CD 1 Track 55

Example 2   CD 1 Track 56

Example 3   CD 1 Track 57

Ear Tests

Example 4
CD 1 Track 58

Example 5
CD 1 Track 59

Example 6
CD 1 Track 60

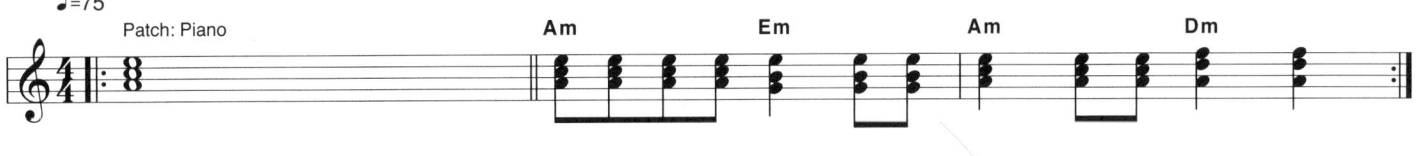

Ear Tests

Grade 3 | Test 1 | Melodic Recall

You will be asked to play back using the piano patch on your keyboard a four-bar melody composed from either the C minor pentatonic or G minor pentatonic scales. You will be given the tonic note and told the starting note and you will hear the test twice with a drum backing. There will then be a short break for you to practise the test and then the test will recommence and you will be required to play the melody with the drum backing. This test is continuous.

Example 1   CD 2 Track 1

Gm / B♭

Example 2   CD 2 Track 2

Example 3   CD 2 Track 3

Ear Tests

Example 4   CD 2 Track 4

Example 5   CD 2 Track 5

Example 6   CD 2 Track 6

Ear Tests

Grade 3 | Test 2 | Chord and Rhythm Recall

You will be asked to play back using the piano patch on your keyboard a four-bar rhythmic chord sequence on your keyboard. You will be told the tonic chord, first chord and the inversion. You will hear the rhythmic chord sequence made up of chords I, IV and V^7 in the key of D major or A major played twice with a drum backing. There will then be a short break for you to practise the test and then the test will recommence and you will be required to play the rhythmic chord sequence to the drum backing. This test is continuous.

Example 1   CD 2 Track 7

Example 2   CD 2 Track 8

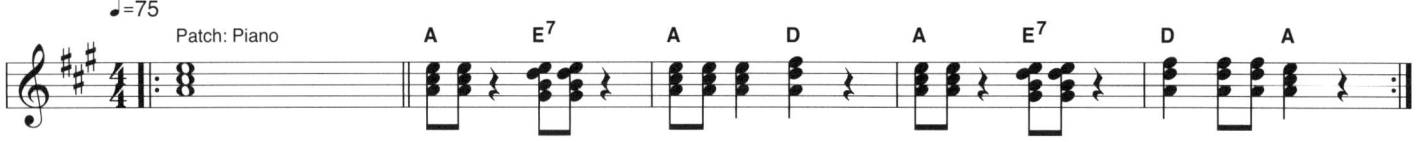

Example 3   CD 2 Track 9

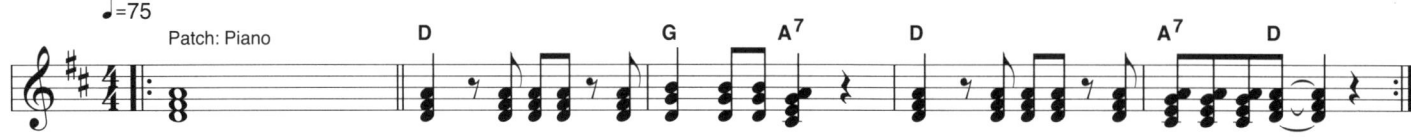

Ear Tests

Example 4 CD 2 Track 10

Example 5 CD 2 Track 11

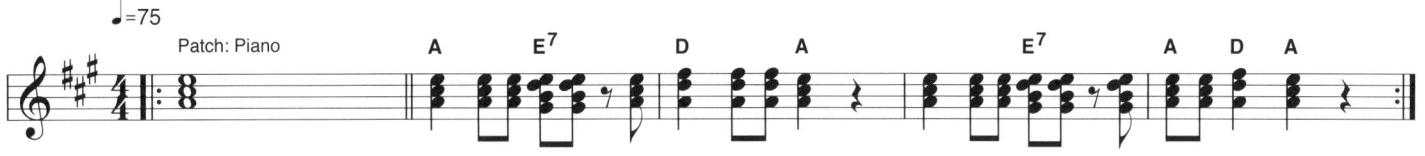

Example 6 CD 2 Track 12

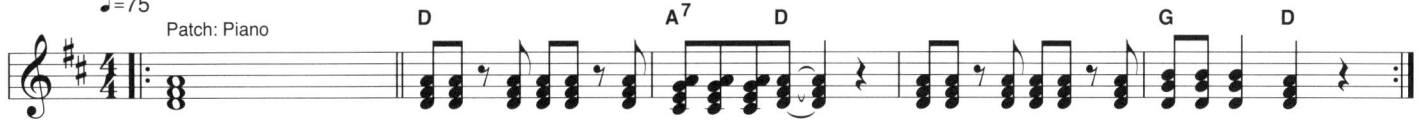

Ear Tests

Grade 4 | Test 1 | Melodic Recall

You will be asked to play back using the piano or electric piano patch on your keyboard a four-bar melody composed from either the D major or E major scales. You will be given the tonic note and told the starting note and you will hear the test twice with a drum backing. There will be a short break for you to practise the test and then the test will recommence and you will be required to play the melody with the drum backing using the patch indicated on the CD. This test is continuous.

Example 1   CD 2 Track 13

Example 2   CD 2 Track 14

Example 3   CD 2 Track 15

Ear Tests

Example 4   CD 2 Track 16

Example 5   CD 2 Track 17

Example 6   CD 2 Track 18

Ear Tests

Grade 4 | Test 2 | Chord and Rhythm Recall

You will be asked to play back using either the piano or electric piano patch on your keyboard a four-bar rhythmic chord sequence. You will be told the tonic chord, the first chord and chord inversion and you will hear the rhythmic chord sequence made up of chords I, ii^7, IV and V^7 in the key of either D major or E major played twice with a drum backing. There will then be a short break for you to practise and then the test will recommence and you will be required to play the rhythmic chord sequence to the drum backing using the patch indicated on the CD. This test is continuous.

Example 1   CD 2 Track 19

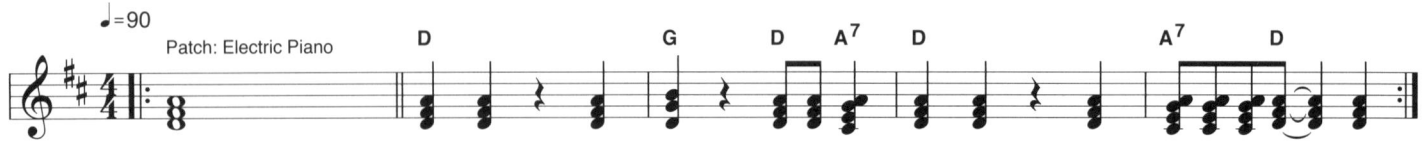

Example 2   CD 2 Track 20

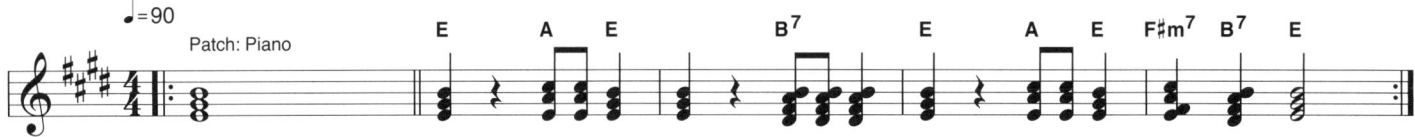

Example 3   CD 2 Track 21

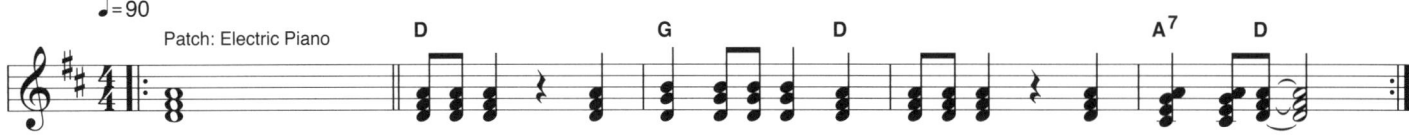

Ear Tests

Example 4　　　　　　　　　　　　　　　　　　　　　　　　　　　　　　　　CD 2 Track 22

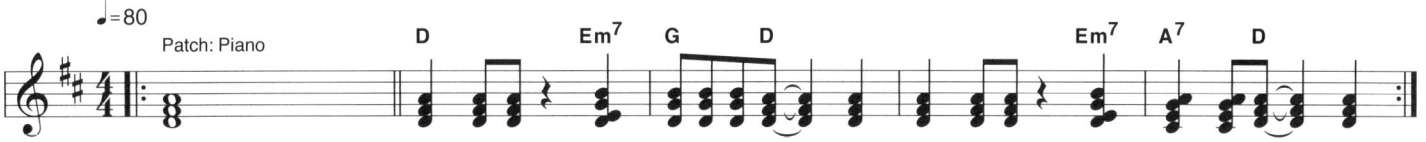

Example 5　　　　　　　　　　　　　　　　　　　　　　　　　　　　　　　　CD 2 Track 23

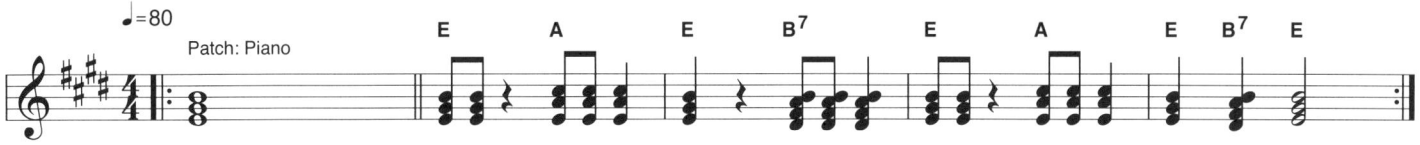

Example 6　　　　　　　　　　　　　　　　　　　　　　　　　　　　　　　　CD 2 Track 24

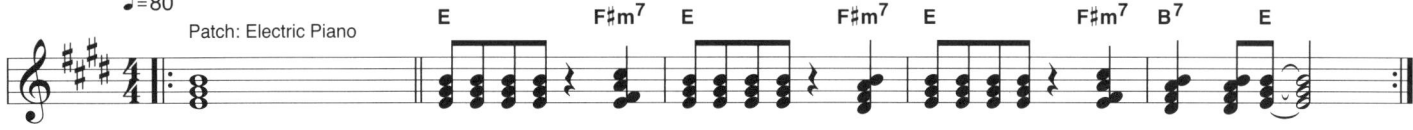

Ear Tests

Grade 5 | Test 1 | Melodic Recall

You will be asked to play back using either the piano or electric piano patch on your keyboard a four-bar bass melody composed from either the G blues or B blues scales. You will be given the tonic note and told the starting note and you will hear the test twice with a drum backing. There will then be a short break for you to practise the test and then the test will recommence and you will be required play the melody with the drum backing using the patch indicated on the CD. This test is continuous.

Example 1   CD 2 Track 25

Example 2   CD 2 Track 26

Example 3   CD 2 Track 27

Ear Tests

Example 4 CD 2 Track 28

Example 5 CD 2 Track 29

Example 6 CD 2 Track 30

Ear Tests

Grade 5 | Test 2 | Chord and Rhythm Recall

You will be asked to play back using either the piano or electric piano patch on your keyboard a four-bar rhythmic chord sequence. You will be told the tonic chord, the first chord and the inversion, and you will hear the rhythmic chord sequence made up of chords i7, iv and v in a G blues or B blues played twice with a drum backing. There will then be a short break for you to practise the test and then the test will recommence and you will be required play the rhythmic chord sequence to the drum backing using the patch indicated on the CD. This test is continuous.

Example 1   CD 2 Track 31

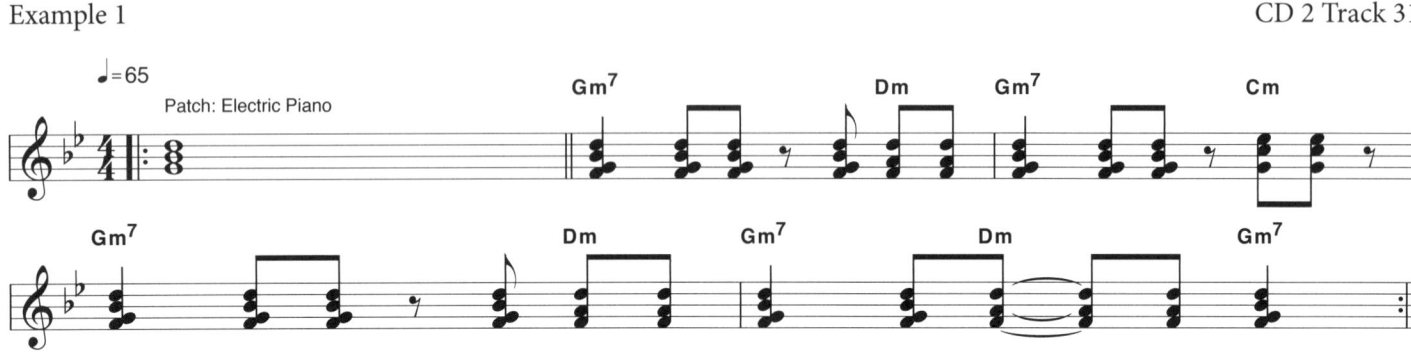

Example 2   CD 2 Track 32

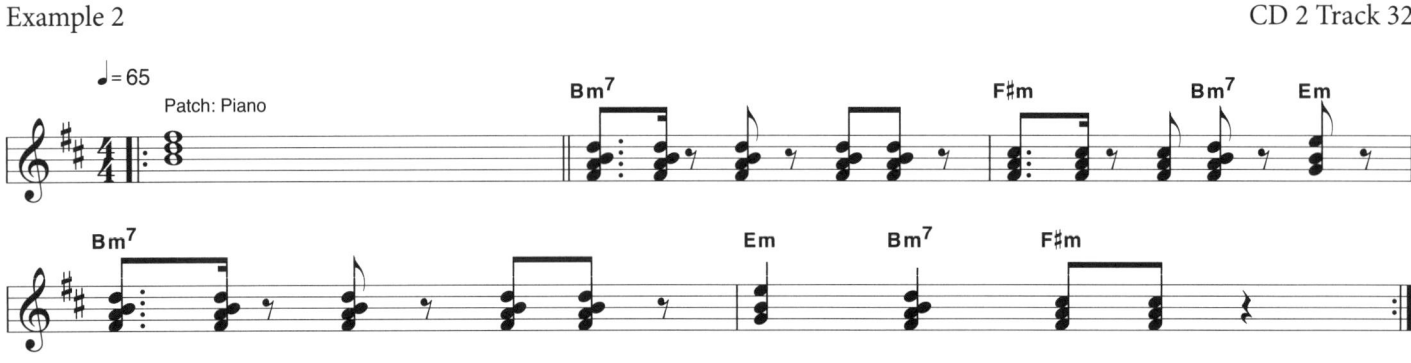

Example 3   CD 2 Track 33

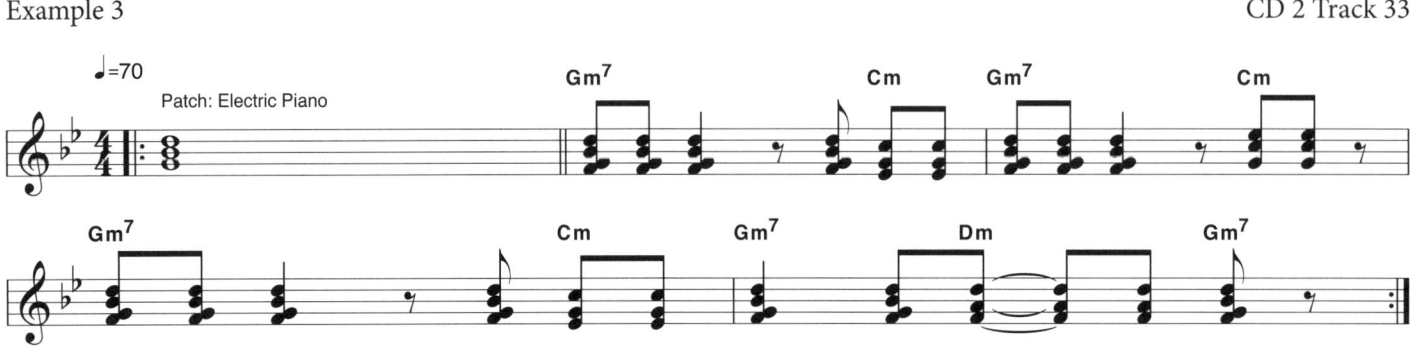

Ear Tests

Example 4
CD 2 Track 34

Example 5
CD 2 Track 35

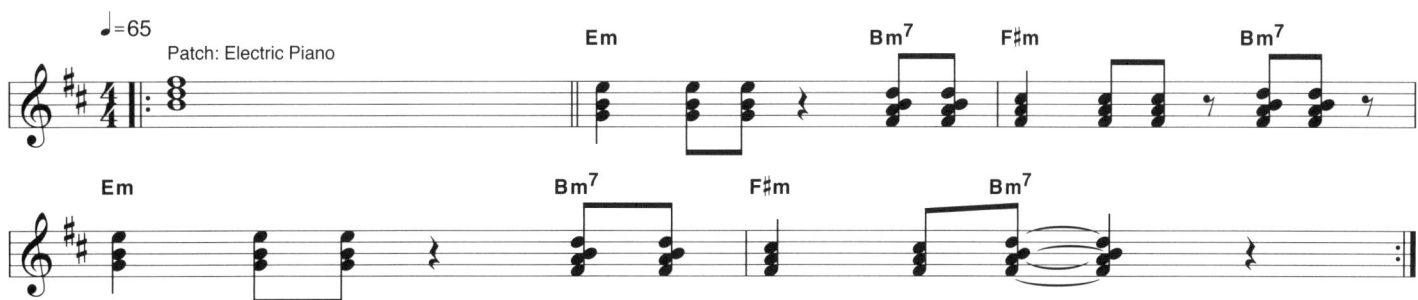

Example 6
CD 2 Track 36

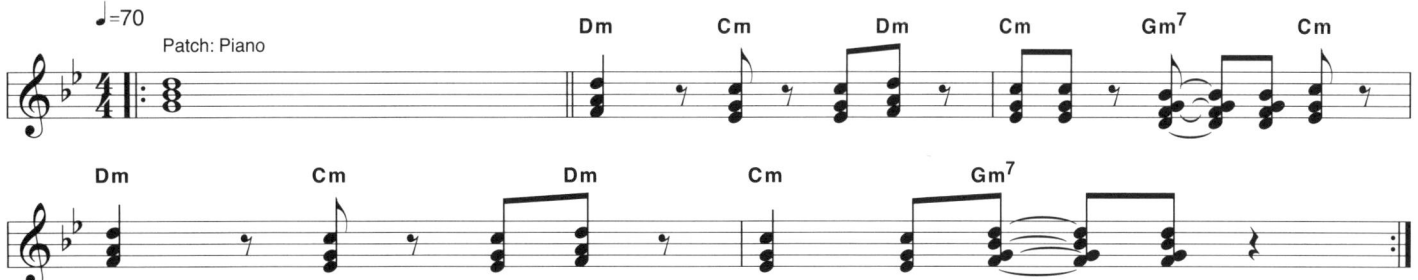

General Musicianship Questions

Each Rockschool grade exam ends with five questions asked by the examiner. The examiner will ask you these questions using a piece played by you as a starting point. In Grades Debut–5, you will be asked questions in two main areas: (i) music notation and (ii) knowledge of the keyboard.

Here are some sample questions that are typically asked by Rockschool's examiners grade by grade, along with sample answers typically given by candidates. As a general rule, in Grades 1–3, examiners will ask candidates 4 questions on the music notation and one instrument question. In Grades 4–5 the instrument knowledge questions may also include selecting and changing patches. Please note that these are indicative questions and some may be asked in more than one grade.

Debut

The theory questions here refer to the performance piece 'The Nick Of Time' on page 18 of the BBK Debut candidate book.

Q: What is the pitch of the first note in the right hand part?
A: B

Q: How many beats is the first note of the left hand part?
A: Two beats

Q: What is "4/4" and what does it mean?
A: It is the time signature and specifies how many beats are in each bar.

Q: What is the value of the first note of the left hand part in bar 2?
A: Half note or minim.

Instrumental Question:
Q: How are the black notes grouped on the keyboard?
A: They are grouped in twos and threes.

Grade 1

The theory questions in this section are based on the performance piece 'Crescent City' Voodoo on page 10 of the BBK Grade 1 candidate book.

Q: What does 4/4 mean?
A: Four quarter notes per bar

Q How many beats is the first note in the right-hand part worth?
A: One beat

Q: What is the pitch of the first note of the right hand part?
A: D

Q: What is the difference between a major and minor chord?
A: A major chord sounds 'happy' and a minor chord sounds 'sad' OR A major chord has a major third and a minor chord has a minor third.

Instrumental Question:
Q: Where is the on/off switch on your keyboard?

Grade 2

The theory questions here refer to the performance piece 'Like It Is' on page 18 of the BBK Grade 2 candidate book.

Q: What does *mf* mean
A: Moderately loud

Q: What does the flat at the beginning of the piece mean?
A: It is the key signature and indicates that every B note should be played as a B♭.

Q: What are the signs at the start of bar 1 and the end of bar 12?
A: Repeat signs

Q: How is a major chord constructed?
A: With the 1st, 3rd and 5th notes of the major scale

Instrumental Question:
Q: Show me how you selected the patch for this song.

Grade 3

The theory questions here refer to the performance piece 'Hazi Taxi' on page 14 of the BBK Grade 3 candidate book.

Q: What do the dots above the notes in bar 8 mean?
A: Play the note short and detached or staccato

Q: What are the values of the notes in bar 18?
A: Triplets

Q: What is the key signature of this piece?
A: E major

Q: How is a minor chord constructed?
A: With the 1st, ♭3rd and 5th notes of the major scale

Instrumental Question:
Q: Identify two of the main makes of keyboard
A: Roland and Yamaha

General Musicianship Questions

Grade 4

The theory questions here refer to the performance piece, 'My Goodness' on page 26 of the BBK Grade 5 candidate book.

Q: What are the pitches of the three-note chord on beat one of the right-hand part of bar 5?
A: A♭, C and E♭

Q: What does *mp* mean?
A: Moderately quiet.

Q: What does the line connecting the two B♭ notes in bar 11 mean?
A: These are tied notes. The first note is played and held for the duration of both notes.

Q: How is a minor seventh chord constructed?
A: With the root, major 3rd, perfect 5th and flattened 7th notes of a major scale.

Instrumental Question:
Q: How do you select and store patches in your keyboard?

Grade 5

The theory questions here refer to Sidewinder on page 30 of the BBK Grade 5 candidate book.

Q: What is the key signature of the piece?
A: One sharp, F♯: E minor

Q: What is the pitch of the first two notes in the right hand part of bar 20?
A: E and G

Q: What do *mp* and *f* mean?
A: Moderately softly (mezzo piano) and loud (forte)

Q: How would you construct a major⁷ chord?
A: With the 1st, 3rd, 5th and 7th notes of a major scale.

Instrumental Question:
Q: What are the different playing techniques required for playing the pad and power synth in this piece?